# Instant Omni Air Fryer Toaster Oven Cookbook

D1500471

## 100 Quick, Easy and Delicious Instant Omni Toaster Oven Recipes for Healthy Cook's Kitchen

Jeanette Hopkins

# Table of Contents

# Introduction

The Instant Omni plus toaster oven is the perfect oven to use in the home kitchen or in a professional setting. Whether you are an expert or a beginner, its range of cooking programs, and easy to use control panel will definitely make cooking a convenient job for you. This toaster oven is a breeze for those who want to cook large servings at a time. It is an advanced version of the previously launched Instant Omni, and it provides greater capacity and additional cooking functions.

Advantages of Using Instant Omni

The following features of the Instant Omni make this toaster a must to keep cooking appliance:

## Eight Smart functions

This toaster oven combines all the cooking functions of an oven, broiler, air fryer, and a toaster. Imagine you have one single appliance that can carry out all such functions. Each smart program comes with a preset temperature and timer settings, which are also adjustable as per the needs. The seven cooking programs of the Instant Omni toaster oven includes:

- Air Fry
- Broil
- Bake
- Roast
- Toast
- Dehydrate
- Slow Cook
- Reheat

## Two cooking modes

One feature that makes Instant Omni a toaster oven different from other toaster ovens is its two cooking modes. This feature is rare or impossible to find in other toaster ovens. There are two cooking modes which can be used to cook different types of meals. The two modes are:

## 1. Rotate

Using this mode, a user can cook or roast its chicken, duck, or any other meat on the rotisserie. The heat is provided to the food as it rotates on the rotisserie stick.

## 2. Convection

This mode is suitable for all other cooking functions in which food is placed in a fixed position. The heat is produced and regulated inside the oven through convection.

## XL Capacity

The size of Instant Omni takes it to the top of the list when compared to other toaster ovens. Its great capacity to accommodate all food types, whether you want to cook a whole chicken inside or what to Air fryer a large batch of French fries, the appliance is capable of carrying them all at a time. So, it is perfect to use for large families. The XL capacity of the Instant Omni can cook the following in a single layer:

- 12" Pizza
- Six Toast Slices
- Easy to Read Display screen

The display panel of the Instant Omni is easy to understand. It has a display at the center, which is surrounded by the touch keys for all the smart programs, the cooking modes, and the on/off functions. There are separate knobs attached at the two ends of the touch panel, which can be used to adjust the cooking programs, time, and temperature manually.

## Intuitive Customizable Programs

All the smart programs of Instant Omni are customizable. Even when the cooking program is running, the settings can be changed using the temperature and time knobs. The adjustable programs allow the users to switch from one cooking settings to another with its super flexible heating system.

Even-Heat: Toasts Both Sides

Due to its convection heating mechanism, the Instant Omni toaster oven is capable of heating the food from all sides. This feature ensures even heating. When bread slices or bagels are toasted inside this toaster oven, they are cooked both from the top and the bottom. Without flipping a single slice, a user can get evenly cooked and crispy toasts.

Unboxing the Instant Omni Plus Toaster Oven

When it comes to electric appliances, it is important to inspect all the parts of the appliance before giving it a test run. The Instant Omni toaster oven comes with the following basic elements and the accessories.

- The Oven Base unit
- Rack tray
- Crumb Tray
- Oven Door
- Rotisserie Catch
- Rotisserie Spit & Forks Rotisserie Lift
- Air Fry Basket
- Baking pan
- Baking trays
- Power plug

Inside the Instant Omni plus oven, there are three grooves on both sides. These grooves are used to insert three rack trays in the oven. The uppermost grooves can be used to insert the trays when the food needs to be broiled. The center grooves are for Air frying and Roasting purposes. The lowermost level is used to place the food which needs to be baked, reheated, or dehydrated. Crumb tray is inserted at the bottom to protect the bottom of the oven from the food particle during cooking. The rotisserie stick can be inserted and used to fix the meat of chicken. This stick can be fixed on the inner side of the center portion of the oven into the rotisserie catch. Air fryer basket can be placed on the lower rack when required.

**Control Panel**

The control panel of the appliance is fixed on the front top portion of the oven. The center black panel consists of the touch screen, which shows all the functions. This panel is placed in between two knobs which are used to adjust the time and cooking temperature:

Smart Program Keys: The seven smart program keys are located at the bottom of the black panel. Any of the programs can be selected by rotating the preset dial.

Display: right above the keys, there is a display which lights in blue colored figures indicating the time, temperature, and other indicators like Start, Cancel, Door, Warm, Flip or turn, etc.

Cooking Modes: There are two keys to the cooking modes, indicated by the: Rotate and Convection marks.

Start and Cancel Key: At the two corners of the display screen, there are keys to start or cancel a selected program.

Dials: The Temp/time dial can be used to adjust the cooking time and temperature. Rotate the dial to the right to increase the value of rotate it to the left to decrease the values. The Preset dial is used to switch the cooking modes.

**Featured Cooking Functions and Programs**

There are eight smart programs that give different cooking modes to the users, which are as follow:

**1. Air Fry**

Using this program, to cook oil-free, crispy food, whether its coated meat or fries, everything can be fried in its Air fryer basket.

**2. Toast**

The temp/time dial that is used to set the temperature and cooking time can be used to select the bread slices and their brownness when they need to be toasted using the Toast cooking program of the Instant Omni toaster oven.

**3. Bake**

It is used to bake cakes, brownies, or bread in quick time.

### 4. Broil

The broiler's settings provide direct top-down heat to crisp meat, melt cheese, and caramelize vegetables and fruits. It has the default highest temperature, that is 450 degrees F.

### 5. Roast

This cooking program is suitable for roasting meats and vegetables.

### 6. Slow Cooker

The Slow Cook program lets you adjust greater cooking time and lowest temperatures based on the requirements.

### 7. Reheat

Using this mode, the users can warm up leftover food without overcooking the food.

### 8. Dehydrate

Low-temperature heat is regulated to effectively remove moisture from foods, thus giving perfect crispy veggie chips, jerky, and dehydrated fruits.

### Meal Preparation and Cooking Method

- Cooking all sorts of meals in the Instant Omni Plus is like a breeze. Following are steps to prepare a fresh and good meal in no time:
- Prepare the Appliance
- Plugin your appliance, and you will the display lighting up instantly. Make sure the appliance is placed over a flat and stable surface. Place the crumb tray inside the oven at the bottom.

### Set the Accessories

Think about what cooking modes you are going to use and then select the accessories accordingly. Set the steel racks in any of the three portions to set the food. Use Air fryer basket, or the baking pans or tray, or fix the rotisserie stick in the rotisserie catch.

### Preheat when Needed

To preheat the toaster oven, select the required cooking program and temperature. The preset dial on the left side of the screen is used to select the program then adjust the time and temperature using the temp/time dial. Also, select the cooking mode: rotate: to cook food rotisserie or the convection mode to cook other food. The oven will then go into the preheating mode upon pressing the start button; at this point, the timer will not start ticking.

### Place the Food Inside

When the appliance is preheated, the display will indicate that along with a beep. Now you can place the food inside and then close the oven door. If you don't want to preheat the appliance, then you can also set the cooking modes, temperature, and time after placing the food. When its food is all set and ready to cook, then you can hit the start the button, and it will initiate cooking.

### Flip and turn the food

When the food requires to be tossed, turned, or flipped, then the LED display will the word FLIP on the screen. The cooking function is paused when you open the oven door and flip the food. Now you can resume the cooking by pressing the start button. The appliance beeps at the end of the cooking program. It's time to serve the food.

### Cleaning and Storage

The instant Omni toaster oven must be cleaned after every cooking session like any other cooking appliance. It is important to keep the inside of the oven germs free all the time. The food particles that are stuck at the base or on the walls of the oven should be cleaned after every session using the following steps:

Unplug the Instant Omni toaster oven and allow it to cool down completely. Keep the door open while it cools down.

Now remove all the trays, dripping pan, the steel racks, and other accessories from inside the oven.

Place the removable parts of the oven in the dishwasher and wash them thoroughly.

Once these accessories are washed, all of them dry out completely.

Meanwhile, take a clean and slightly damp cloth to clean the inside of the oven.

Wipe all the internal walls of the oven using this cloth. Be gentle while you do the wiping.

Now use another cloth to clean the exterior of the appliance. Wipe off all the surfaces, especially the touchscreen.

Now that everything is clean, you can place the steel racks and dripping pan back to their position for the next session of cooking.

For cleaning, do not immerse your appliance in the water directly.

To clean the power plug, use a dry piece of cloth to remove the dirt.

## How to Use the Instant Omni Toaster Oven

1. Open the door of the oven. Put the cooking pan in the
2. cooking chamber (at the bottom level).
3. Insert the power cord into the power source (120v). You will see 'OFF' on the display indicating that your oven is in the standby mode.
4. Tap on 'Air fry' mode key.
5. Adjust the time dial (+) and (-) to a cooking time of your choice (e.g. 20 minutes).
6. Tap on the green 'Start' key to begin the cooking process. When the oven is on the preheat mode, the display shows 'ON'
7. When the oven reaches the preset temperature, the countdown
8. begins automatically.
9. Halfway into the cooking process, the alarm sound will beep to indicate 'Turn Food.' (This implies that you should flip your food). This 'Turn food' is only active when using Roast, Bake and Air fry functions. The cooking continues after 10 seconds whether you turned the food or not.
10. When the specific program has been completed, you will see 'End' on the display. The fan comes up to cool the oven automatically. The omni toaster oven sends a reminder at 5, 20 and 60 minutes' intervals after cooking. This is to inform you that the food is ready.

## Basic tips

1. You can press and hold the temperature knob for 3 seconds. This will make it switch from Celsius to Fahrenheit. You will hear a beep sound. If you hold it again for another 3 seconds, it will go back to Celsius.
2. If you press and hold the time knob firmly for 3 seconds, it will activate the oven light.
3. To cancel a default setting on a/all the modes, just press and hold the 'cancel' for 3 seconds. The default is no longer active.
4. To deactivate the beeping sound, hold the temperature and time knob at the same time. You will see SOFF meaning that the sound is OFF. To activate the sound again, hold the time and temperature knob for 3 seconds.

## Safety Precautions/Cleaning the Instant Omni

1. Always clean your omni after using it.
2. Lower your baking tray to the middle position for even circulation of heat.
3. Unplug your instant omni when not in use.
4. Also, never put anything on top of your oven because it will affect the temperature gauge.

# Breakfast

## 1. Milky Scrambled Eggs

Preparation Time: 10 minutes
Cooking time: 9 minutes
Servings: 2
**INGREDIENTS:**

- ¾ cup milk
- 4 eggs
- 8 grape tomatoes, halved
- ½ cup Parmesan cheese, grated
- 1 tablespoon butter
- Salt and black pepper, to taste

**DIRECTIONS:**

1. Preheat the Air fryer to 360 o F and grease an Air fryer pan with butter.
2. Whisk together eggs with milk, salt and black pepper in a bowl.
3. Transfer the egg mixture into the prepared pan and place in the Air fryer.
4. Cook for about 6 minutes and stir in the grape tomatoes and cheese.
5. Cook for about 3 minutes and serve warm.

**NUTRITION:** Calories: 351 Fat: 22g Carbohydrates: 25.2g Protein: 26.4g

## 2. Yummy Savory French Toasts

Preparation Time: 10 minutes
Cooking time: 4 minutes
Servings: 2
**INGREDIENTS:**

- ¼ cup chickpea flour
- 3 tablespoons onion, chopped finely
- 2 teaspoons green chili, seeded and chopped finely
- Water, as required
- 4 bread slices
- ½ teaspoon red chili powder
- ¼ teaspoon ground turmeric
- ¼ teaspoon ground cumin
- Salt, to taste

**DIRECTIONS:**

1. Preheat the Air fryer to 375 o F and line an Air fryer pan with a foil paper.
2. Mix together all the ingredients in a large bowl except the bread slices.
3. Spread the mixture over both sides of the bread slices and transfer into the Air fryer pan.
4. Cook for about 4 minutes and remove from the Air fryer to serve.

**NUTRITION:** Calories: 151 Fat: 2.3g Carbohydrates: 26.7g Protein: 6.5g

## 3. Crispy Potato Rosti

Preparation Time: 10 minutes
Cooking time: 15 minutes
Servings: 2
**INGREDIENTS:**

- ½ pound russet potatoes, peeled and grated roughly

- 1 tablespoon chives, chopped finely
- 2 tablespoons shallots, minced
- 1/8 cup cheddar cheese
- 3.5 ounces smoked salmon, cut into slices
- 2 tablespoons sour cream
- 1 tablespoon olive oil
- Salt and black pepper, to taste

**DIRECTIONS:**
1. Preheat the Air fryer to 365 o F and grease a pizza pan with the olive oil.
2. Mix together potatoes, shallots, chives, cheese, salt and black pepper in a large bowl until well combined.
3. Transfer the potato mixture into the prepared pizza pan and place in the Air fryer basket.
4. Cook for about 15 minutes and dish out in a platter.
5. Cut the potato rosti into wedges and top with smoked salmon slices and sour cream to serve.

**NUTRITION:** Calories: 327 Fat: 20.2g Carbohydrates: 23.3g Protein: 15.3g

## 4. Toasties and Sausage in Egg Pond

Preparation Time: 10 minutes
Cooking time: 22 minutes
Servings: 2

**INGREDIENTS:**

- 3 eggs
- 2 cooked sausages, sliced
- 1 bread slice, cut into sticks
- 1/8 cup mozzarella cheese, grated
- 1/8 cup Parmesan cheese, grated
- ¼ cup cream

**DIRECTIONS:**
1. Preheat the Air fryer to 365 o F and grease 2 ramekins lightly.
2. Whisk together eggs with cream in a bowl and place in the ramekins.
3. Stir in the bread and sausage slices in the egg mixture and top with cheese.
4. Transfer the ramekins in the Air fryer basket and cook for about 22 minutes.
5. Dish out and serve warm.

**NUTRITION:** Calories: 261 Fat: 18.8g Carbohydrates: 4.2g Protein: 18.3g

## 5. Banana Bread

Preparation Time: 10 minutes
Cooking time: 20 minutes
Servings: 8

**INGREDIENTS:**

- 1 1/3 cups flour
- 1 teaspoon baking soda
- 1 teaspoon baking powder
- ½ cup milk
- 3 bananas, peeled and sliced
- 2/3 cup sugar
- 1 teaspoon ground cinnamon
- 1 teaspoon salt

- ½ cup olive oil

**DIRECTIONS:**
1. Preheat the Air fryer to 330 o F and grease a loaf pan.
2. Mix together all the dry ingredients with the wet ingredients to form a dough.
3. Place the dough into the prepared loaf pan and transfer into an air fryer basket.
4. Cook for about 20 minutes and remove from air fryer.
5. Cut the bread into desired size slices and serve warm.

**NUTRITION:** Calories: 295 Fat: 13.3g Carbohydrates: 44g Protein: 3.1g

## 6. Peanut Butter Banana Bread

Preparation Time: 15 minutes
Cooking time: 40 minutes
Servings: 6

**INGREDIENTS:**
- 1 cup plus 1 tablespoon all-purpose flour
- 1¼ teaspoons baking powder
- 1 large egg
- 2 medium ripe bananas, peeled and mashed
- ¾ cup walnuts, roughly chopped
- ¼ teaspoon salt
- 1/3 cup granulated sugar
- ¼ cup canola oil
- 2 tablespoons creamy peanut butter
- 2 tablespoons sour cream
- 1 teaspoon vanilla extract

**DIRECTIONS:**
1. Preheat the Air fryer to 330 o F and grease a non-stick baking dish.
2. Mix together the flour, baking powder and salt in a bowl.
3. Whisk together egg with sugar, canola oil, sour cream, peanut butter and vanilla extract in a bowl.
4. Stir in the bananas and beat until well combined.
5. Now, add the flour mixture and fold in the walnuts gently.
6. Mix until combined and transfer the mixture evenly into the prepared baking dish.
7. Arrange the baking dish in an Air fryer basket and cook for about 40 minutes.
8. Remove from the Air fryer and place onto a wire rack to cool.
9. Cut the bread into desired size slices and serve.

**NUTRITION:** Calories: 384 Fat: 2.6g Carbohydrates: 39.3g Protein: 8.9g

## 7. Flavorful Bacon Cups

Preparation Time: 10 minutes
Cooking time: 15 minutes
Servings: 6

**INGREDIENTS:**
- 6 bacon slices
- 6 bread slices
- 1 scallion, chopped
- 3 tablespoons green bell pepper, seeded and chopped
- 6 eggs
- 2 tablespoons low-fat mayonnaise

**DIRECTIONS:**
1. Preheat the Air fryer to 375 o F and grease 6 cups muffin tin with cooking spray.
2. Place each bacon slice in a prepared muffin cup.
3. Cut the bread slices with round cookie cutter and place over the bacon slices.
4. Top with bell pepper, scallion and mayonnaise evenly and crack 1 egg in each muffin cup.
5. Place in the Air fryer and cook for about 15 minutes.
6. Dish out and serve warm.

**NUTRITION:** Calories: 260 Fat: 18g Carbohydrates: 6.9g Protein: 16.7g

## 8. Stylish Ham Omelet

Preparation Time: 10 minutes
Cooking time: 30 minutes
Servings: 2

**INGREDIENTS:**

- 4 small tomatoes, chopped
- 4 eggs
- 2 ham slices
- 1 onion, chopped
- 2 tablespoons cheddar cheese
- Salt and black pepper, to taste

**DIRECTIONS:**
1. Preheat the Air fryer to 390 o F and grease an Air fryer pan.
2. Place the tomatoes in the Air fryer pan and cook for about 10 minutes.
3. Heat a nonstick skillet on medium heat and add onion and ham.
4. Stir fry for about 5 minutes and transfer into the Air fryer pan.
5. Whisk together eggs, salt and black pepper in a bowl and pour in the Air fryer pan.
6. Set the Air fryer to 335 o F and cook for about 15 minutes.
7. Dish out and serve warm.

**NUTRITION:** Calories: 255 Fat: 13.9g Carbohydrates: 14.1gProtein: 19.7g

## 9. Aromatic Potato Hash

Preparation Time: 10 minutes
Cooking time: 42 minutes
Servings: 4

**INGREDIENTS:**

- 2 teaspoons butter, melted
- 1 medium onion, chopped
- ½ of green bell pepper, seeded and chopped
- 1½ pound russet potatoes, peeled and cubed
- 5 eggs, beaten
- ½ teaspoon dried thyme, crushed
- ½ teaspoon dried savory, crushed
- Salt and black pepper, to taste

**DIRECTIONS:**
1. Preheat the Air fryer to 390 o F and grease an Air fryer pan with melted butter.
2. Put onion and bell pepper in the Air fryer pan and cook for about 5 minutes.
3. Add the potatoes, thyme, savory, salt and black pepper and cook for about 30 minutes.
4. Meanwhile, heat a greased skillet on medium heat and stir in the beaten eggs.
5. Cook for about 1 minute on each side and remove from the skillet.

6. Cut it into small pieces and transfer the egg pieces into the Air fryer pan.
7. Cook for about 5 more minutes and serve warm.

**NUTRITION:** Calories: 229 Fat: 7.6g Carbohydrates: 30.8g Protein: 10.3g

## 10. Healthy Tofu Omelet

Preparation Time: 10 minutes
Cooking time: 29 minutes
Servings: 2

**INGREDIENTS:**

- ¼ of onion, chopped
- 12-ounce silken tofu, pressed and sliced
- 3 eggs, beaten
- 1 tablespoon chives, chopped
- 1 garlic clove, minced
- 2 teaspoons olive oil
- Salt and black pepper, to taste

**DIRECTIONS:**

1. Preheat the Air fryer to 355 o F and grease an Air fryer pan with olive oil.
2. Add onion and garlic to the greased pan and cook for about 4 minutes.
3. Add tofu, mushrooms and chives and season with salt and black pepper.
4. Beat the eggs and pour over the tofu mixture.
5. Cook for about 25 minutes, poking the eggs twice in between.
6. Dish out and serve warm.

**NUTRITION:** Calories: 248 Fat: 15.9g Carbohydrates: 6.5g Protein: 20.4g

# Mains

## 11. Chicken Pot Pie

Preparation Time: 10 minutes
Cooking Time: 17 minutes
Servings: 6

**INGREDIENTS:**

- 2 tbsp olive oil
- 1-pound chicken breast cubed
- 1 tbsp garlic powder
- 1 tbsp thyme
- 1 tbsp pepper
- 1 cup chicken broth
- 12 oz. bag frozen mixed vegetables
- 4 large potatoes cubed
- 10 oz. Can cream of chicken soup
- 1 cup heavy cream
- 1 pie crust
- 1 egg 1 tbsp water

**DIRECTIONS:**

1. Hit Sauté on the Instant Pot Duo Crispy and add chicken and olive oil.
2. Sauté chicken for 5 minutes then stir in spices.
3. Pour in the broth along with vegetables and cream of chicken soup
4. Put on the pressure-cooking lid and seal it.
5. Hit the "Pressure Button" and select 10 minutes of cooking time, then press "Start."
6. Once the Instant Pot Duo beeps, do a quick release and remove its lid.
7. Remove the lid and stir in cream.
8. Hit sauté and cook for 2 minutes.
9. Enjoy!

**NUTRITION:** Calories: 568 Fat: 31.1g Carbohydrates: 50.8g Fiber: 3.9g Protein: 23.4g

## 12. Chicken Casserole

Preparation Time: 10 Minutes
Cooking Time: 9 minutes
Servings: 6

**INGREDIENTS:**

- 3 cup chicken, shredded
- 12 oz. bag egg noodles
- 1/2 large onion
- 1/2 cup chopped carrots
- 1/4 cup frozen peas
- 1/4 cup frozen broccoli pieces
- 2 stalks celery chopped
- 5 cup chicken broth
- 1 teaspoon garlic powder
- salt and pepper to taste
- 1 cup cheddar cheese, shredded

- 1 package French's onions
- 1/4 c sour cream
- 1 can cream of chicken and mushroom soup

**DIRECTIONS:**
1. Add chicken, broth, black pepper, salt, garlic powder, vegetables, and egg noodles to the Instant Pot Duo.
2. Put on the pressure-cooking lid and seal it.
3. Hit the "Pressure Button" and select 4 minutes of cooking time, then press "Start."
4. Once the Instant Pot Duo beeps, do a quick release and remove its lid.
5. Stir in cheese, 1/3 of French's onions, can of soup and sour cream.
6. Mix well and spread the remaining onion top.
7. Put on the Air Fryer lid and seal it.
8. Hit the "Air fryer Button" and select 5 minutes of cooking time, then press "Start."
9. Once the Instant Pot Duo beeps, remove its lid.
10. Serve.

**NUTRITION:** Calories: 494 Fat: 19.1g Carbohydrates: 29g Fiber: 2.6g Protein: 48.9g

## 13. **Ranch Chicken Wings**

Preparation Time: 10 minutes
Cooking Time: 35 minutes
Servings: 6

**INGREDIENTS:**
- 12 chicken wings
- 1 tablespoon olive oil
- 1 cup chicken broth
- 1/4 cup butter
- 1/2 cup Red Hot Sauce
- 1/4 teaspoon Worcestershire sauce
- 1 tablespoon white vinegar
- 1/4 teaspoon cayenne pepper
- 1/8 teaspoon garlic powder
- Seasoned salt to taste
- Ranch dressing for dipping Celery for garnish

**DIRECTIONS:**
1. Set the Air Fryer Basket in the Instant Pot Duo and pour the broth in it.
2. Spread the chicken wings in the basket and put on the pressure-cooking lid.
3. Hit the "Pressure Button" and select 10 minutes of cooking time, then press "Start."
4. Meanwhile, prepare the sauce and add butter, vinegar, cayenne pepper, garlic powder, Worcestershire sauce, and hot sauce in a small saucepan.
5. Stir cook this sauce for 5 minutes on medium heat until it thickens.
6. Once the Instant Pot Duo beeps, do a quick release and remove its lid.
7. Remove the wings and empty the Instant Pot Duo.
8. Toss the wings with oil, salt, and black pepper.
9. Set the Air Fryer Basket in the Instant Pot Duo and arrange the wings in it.
10. Put on the Air Fryer lid and seal it.
11. Hit the "Air Fryer Button" and select 20 minutes of cooking time, then press "Start."
12. Once the Instant Pot beeps, remove its lid.
13. Transfer the wings to the sauce and mix well.
14. Serve.

**NUTRITION:** Calories: 414 Fat: 31.6g Carbohydrates 11.2g Fibre: 0.3g Protein: 20.4g

## 14. Tofu Sushi Burrito

Preparation Time: 5 minutes
Cooking Time: 15 minutes
Servings: 2
**INGREDIENTS:**

- ¼ block extra firm tofu, pressed and sliced
- 1 tbsp low-sodium soy sauce
- ¼ tsp ground ginger
- ¼ tsp garlic powder
- Sriracha sauce, to taste
- 2 cups cooked sushi rice
- 2 sheets nori
- Filling:
- ¼ avocado, sliced
- 3 tbsp mango, sliced
- 1 green onion, finely chopped
- 2 tbsp pickled ginger
- 2 tbsp panko breadcrumbs

**DIRECTIONS:**

1. Whisk ginger, garlic, soy sauce, sriracha sauce, and tofu in a large bowl.
2. Let them marinate for 10 minutes then transfer them to the air fryer basket.
3. Return the fryer basket to the air fryer and cook on air fry mode for 15 minutes at 370 degrees F.
4. Toss the tofu cubes after 8 minutes then resume cooking.
5. Spread a nori sheet on a work surface and top it with a layer of sushi rice.
6. Place tofu and half of the other filling ingredients over the rice.
7. Roll the sheet tightly to secure the filling inside.
8. Repeat the same steps to make another sushi roll.
9. Enjoy.

**NUTRITION:** Calories: 372 Fat: 11.8 g Carbohydrates: 45.8 g Fiber: 0.6 g Protein: 34 g

## 15. Rosemary Brussels Sprouts

Preparation Time: 5 minutes
Cooking Time: 13 minutes
Servings: 2
**INGREDIENTS:**

- 3 tbsp olive oil
- 2 garlic cloves, minced
- ½ tsp salt
- ¼ tsp pepper
- 1 lb. Brussels sprouts, trimmed and halved
- ½ cup panko breadcrumbs
- 1 ½ tsp fresh rosemary, minced

**DIRECTIONS:**

1. Let your air fryer preheat at 350 degrees F.
2. Mix oil, garlic, salt, and pepper in a bowl and heat for 30 seconds in the microwave.
3. Add 2 tablespoons of this mixture to the Brussel sprouts in a bowl and mix well to coat.

4. Spread the sprouts in the air fryer basket.
5. Return the fryer basket to the air fryer and cook on air fry mode for 5 minutes at 220 degrees F.
6. Toss the sprouts well and continue air frying for 8 minutes more.
7. Mix the remaining oil mixture with rosemary and breadcrumbs in a bowl.
8. Spread this mixture over the Brussel sprouts and return the basket to the fryer.
9. Air fry them for 5 minutes.
10. Enjoy.

**NUTRITION:** Calories: 246 Fat: 7.4 g Carbohydrates: 9.4 g Fiber: 2.7 g Protein: 37.2 g

## 16. Peach-Bourbon Wings

Preparation Time: 5 minutes
Cooking Time: 14 minutes
Servings: 8

**INGREDIENTS:**

- ½ cup peach preserves
- 1 tbsp brown sugar
- 1 garlic cloves, minced
- ¼ tsp salt
- 2 tbsp white vinegar
- 2 tbsp bourbon
- 1 tsp cornstarch
- 1½ tsp water
- 2 lbs. chicken wings

**DIRECTIONS:**

1. Let your air fryer preheat at 400 degrees F.
2. Add salt, garlic, and brown sugar to a food processor and blend well until smooth.
3. Transfer this mixture to a saucepan and add bourbon, peach preserves, and vinegar.
4. Stir cook this mixture to a boil then reduce heat to a simmer.
5. Cook for 6 minutes until the mixture thickens.
6. Mix cornstarch with water and pour this mixture in the saucepan.
7. Stir cook for 2 minutes until it thickens. Keep ¼ cup of this sauce aside.
8. Place the wings in the air fryer basket and brush them with prepared sauce.
9. Return the fryer basket to the air fryer and cook on air fry mode for 6 minutes at 350 degrees F.
10. Flip the wings and brush them again with the sauce.
11. Air fry the wings for another 8 minutes.
12. Serve with reserved sauce.

**NUTRITION:** Calories 293 Fat: 16 g Carbohydrates: 5.2 g Fiber: 1.9 g Protein: 34.2 g

## 17. Reuben Calzones

Preparation Time: 5 minutes
Cooking Time: 12 minutes
Servings: 4

**INGREDIENTS:**

- 1 tube (13.8 ounces) refrigerated pizza crust
- 4 slices Swiss cheese
- 1 cup sauerkraut, rinsed and well drained
- ½ lb. corned beef, sliced & cooked

**DIRECTIONS:**

1. Let your air fryer preheat at 400 degrees F. Grease the air fryer basket with cooking oil.

2. Spread the pizza crust on a lightly floured surface into a 12-inch square.
3. Slice the crust into four smaller squares.
4. Place one slice of cheese, ¼ of the sauerkraut, and 1 slice corned beef over each square diagonally.
5. Fold the squares in half diagonally to form a triangle and pinch the edges together.
6. Place 2 triangles in the air fryer basket at a time and spray them with cooking oil.
7. Return the fryer basket to the air fryer and cook on air fry mode for 12 minutes at 350 degrees F.
8. Air fry the remaining calzone triangles.
9. Enjoy with fresh salad.

**NUTRITION:** Calories: 604 Fat: 30.6 g Carbohydrates: 31.4 g Fiber: 0.2 g Protein: 54.6 g

## 18. Braised Pork

Preparation Time: 40 minutes
Cooking Time: 40 minutes
Servings: 2

**INGREDIENTS:**

- 1 pound pork loin roast, boneless and cubed
- 2 tablespoons butter, melted and divided
- Salt and black pepper, to taste
- 1 cup chicken stock
- ¼ cup dry white wine
- 1 clove garlic, minced
- ½ teaspoon thyme, chopped
- ½ thyme sprig
- 1 bay leaf
- ¼ yellow onion, chopped
- 1 tablespoon white flour
- ¼ pound red grapes

**DIRECTIONS:**

1. Season pork cubes with salt and pepper. Rub with half the melted butter and put in the air fryer. Cook at 370F for 8 minutes.
2. Meanwhile, heat a pan on the stove with 2 tablespoons of butter over medium heat. Add onion and garlic, and stir-fry for 2 minutes.
3. Add bay leaf, flour, thyme, salt, pepper, stock, and wine. Mix well. Bring to a simmer and take off the heat.
4. Add grapes and pork cubes. Cook in the air fryer at 360F for 30 minutes.
5. Serve.

**NUTRITION:** Calories: 320 Fat: 4g Carbohydrates: 29g Protein: 38g

## 19. Lean Beef with Green Onions

Preparation Time: 10 minutes
Cooking Time: 20 minutes
Servings: 2

**INGREDIENTS:**

- ½ cup green onion, chopped
- ½ cup soy sauce
- ¼ cup water
- 2 tablespoons brown sugar
- 2 tablespoons sesame seeds

- 2 cloves garlic, minced
- ½ teaspoon black pepper
- ½ pound lean beef

**DIRECTIONS:**

1. In a bowl, mix the onion with water, soy sauce, garlic, sugar, sesame seeds, and pepper. Whisk and add meat. Marinate for 10 minutes.
2. Drain beef. Preheat the air fryer to 390F, then cook beef for 20 minutes.
3. Serve.

**NUTRITION:** Calories: 329 Fat: 8g Carbohydrates: 26g Protein: 22g

## 20. Lamb Shanks

Preparation Time: 10 minutes
Cooking Time: 45 minutes
Servings: 2

**INGREDIENTS:**

- 2 lamb shanks
- ½ yellow onion, chopped
- ½ tablespoon olive oil
- 2 teaspoons crushed coriander seeds
- 1 tablespoon white flour
- 2 bay leaves
- 1 teaspoon honey
- 2 ½ ounces dry sherry
- 1 ¼ cups chicken stock
- Salt and pepper, to taste

**DIRECTIONS:**

1. Season the lamb shanks with salt and pepper. Rub with half of the oil and cook in the air fryer at 360F for 10 minutes.
2. Heat up a pan with the rest of the oil over medium-high heat. Add onion and coriander. Stir and cook for 5 minutes.
3. Add salt, pepper, bay leaves, honey, stock, sherry, and flour. Bring to a simmer while stirring, then add the lamb. Mix well.
4. Cook in the air fryer at 360F for 30 minutes.
5. Serve.

**NUTRITION:** Calories: 283 Fat: 4g Carbohydrates: 17g Protein: 26g

# Sides

## 21. Cream Cheese Zucchini

Preparation Time: 20 minutes
Cooking Time: 20-30 minutes
Servings: 4

**INGREDIENTS:**

- 1 lb. Zucchinis; cut into wedges
- 1 green onion; sliced
- 1 cup cream cheese, soft
- 1 tbsp. Butter; melted
- 2 tbsp. Basil; chopped.
- 1 tsp. Garlic powder
- A pinch of salt and black pepper

**DIRECTIONS:**

1. In a pan that fits your air fryer, mix the zucchinis with all the other ingredients, toss, introduce in the air fryer and cook at 370°f for 15 minutes
2. Divide between plates and serve as a side dish.

**NUTRITION:** Calories: 129; Fat: 6g; Fiber: 2g; Carbohydrates: 5g; Protein: 8g

## 22. Roasted Fennel

Preparation Time: 20 minutes
Cooking Time: 20-30 minutes
Servings: 4

**INGREDIENTS:**

- 1 lb. Fennel; cut into small wedges
- 3 tbsp. Olive oil
- 2 tbsp. Sunflower seeds
- Juice of ½ lemon
- Salt and black pepper to taste.

**DIRECTIONS:**

1. Take a bowl and mix the fennel wedges with all the ingredients except the sunflower seeds, put them in your air fryer's basket and cook at 400°f for 15 minutes
2. Divide the fennel between plates, sprinkle the sunflower seeds on top and serve as a side dish.

**NUTRITION:** Calories: 152; Fat: 4g; Fiber: 2g; Carbohydrates: 4g; Protein: 7g

## 23. Mexican Style Cauliflower Bake

Preparation Time: 25 minutes
Cooking Time: 20-30 minutes
Servings: 4

**INGREDIENTS:**

- 2 cups cauliflower florets; roughly chopped.
- 1 red chili pepper; chopped.
- 2 tomatoes; cubed
- 1 avocado, peeled, pitted and sliced
- 4 garlic cloves; minced
- 1 tbsp. Coriander; chopped.

- 1 tbsp. Lime juice
- 1 tbsp. Olive oil
- 1 tsp. Cumin powder
- ½ tsp. Chili powder
- Salt and black pepper to taste.

**DIRECTIONS:**
1. In a pan that fits the air fryer, combine the cauliflower with the other ingredients except the coriander, avocado and lime juice, toss, introduce the pan in the machine and cook at 380°f for 20 minutes
2. Divide between plates, top each serving with coriander, avocado and lime juice and serve as a side dish.

**NUTRITION:** Calories: 187; Fat: 8g; Fiber: 2g; Carbohydrates: 5g; Protein: 7g

## 24. **Brussels Sprouts**
Preparation Time: 15 minutes
Cooking Time: 20-30 minutes
Servings: 4

**INGREDIENTS:**
- 1 lb. Brussels sprouts
- 1 tbsp. Unsalted butter; melted.
- 1 tbsp. Coconut oil

**DIRECTIONS:**
1. Remove all loose leaves from brussels sprouts and cut each in half.
2. Drizzle sprouts with coconut oil and place into the air fryer basket
3. Adjust the temperature to 400 degrees f and set the timer for 10 minutes.
4. You may want to gently stir halfway through the cooking time, depending on how they are beginning to brown
5. When completely cooked, they should be tender with darker caramelized spots.
6. Remove from fryer basket and drizzle with melted butter.
7. Serve immediately.

**NUTRITION:** Calories: 90;Protein: 2.9g; Fiber: 3.2g; Fat: 6.1g; Carbohydrates: 7.5g

## 25. **Roasted Tomatoes**
Preparation Time: 20 minutes
Cooking Time: 20-30 minutes
Servings: 4

**INGREDIENTS:**
- 4 tomatoes; halved
- ½ cup parmesan; grated
- 1 tbsp. Basil; chopped.
- ½ tsp. Onion powder
- ½ tsp. Oregano; dried
- ½ tsp. Smoked paprika
- ½ tsp. Garlic powder
- Cooking spray

**DIRECTIONS:**
1. Take a bowl and mix all the ingredients except the cooking spray and the parmesan.
2. Arrange the tomatoes in your air fryer's pan, sprinkle the parmesan on top and grease with cooking spray
3. Cook at 370°f for 15 minutes, divide between plates and serve.

**NUTRITION:** Calories: 200; Fat: 7g; Fiber: 2g; Carbohydrates: 4g; Protein: 6g

## 26. Cauliflower and Artichokes

Preparation Time: 25 minutes
Cooking Time: 20-30 minutes
Servings: 4

**INGREDIENTS:**

- 2 garlic cloves; minced
- ½ cup chicken stock
- 1 cup cauliflower florets
- 15 oz. Canned artichoke hearts; chopped.
- 1 ½ tbsp. Parsley; chopped.
- 1 tbsp. Olive oil
- 1 tbsp. Parmesan; grated
- Salt and black pepper to taste.

**DIRECTIONS:**

1. In a pan that fits your air fryer, mix all the ingredients except the parmesan and toss.
2. Sprinkle the parmesan on top, introduce the pan in the air fryer and cook at 380°f for 20 minutes
3. Divide between plates and serve as a side dish.

**NUTRITION:** Calories: 195; Fat: 6g; Fiber: 2g; Carbohydrates: 4g; Protein: 8g

## 27. Zucchini Noodles and Sauce

Preparation Time: 20 minutes
Cooking Time: 20-30 minutes
Servings: 4

**INGREDIENTS:**

- 4 zucchinis, cut with a spiralizer
- 1 ½ cups tomatoes, crushed
- 4 garlic cloves; minced
- ¼ cup green onions; chopped.
- 1 tbsp. Olive oil
- 1 tbsp. Basil; chopped.
- Salt and black pepper to taste.

**DIRECTIONS:**

1. In a pan that fits your air fryer, mix zucchini noodles with the other ingredients, toss, introduce in the fryer and cook at 380°f for 15 minutes.
2. Divide between plates and serve as a side dish

**NUTRITION:** Calories: 194; Fat: 7g; Fiber: 2g; Carbohydrates: 4g; Protein: 9g

## 28. Broccoli Mash

Preparation Time: 25 minutes
Cooking Time: 20-30 minutes
Servings: 4

**INGREDIENTS:**

- 20 oz. Broccoli florets
- 3 oz. Butter; melted
- 1 garlic clove; minced
- 4 tbsp. Basil; chopped.

- A drizzle of olive oil
- A pinch of salt and black pepper

**DIRECTIONS:**
1. Take a bowl and mix the broccoli with the oil, salt and pepper, toss and transfer to your air fryer's basket.
2. Cook at 380°f for 20 minutes, cool the broccoli down and put it in a blender
3. Add the rest of the ingredients, pulse, divide the mash between plates and serve as a side dish.

**NUTRITION:** Calories: 200; Fat: 14g; Fiber: 3g; Carbohydrates: 6g;Protein: 7g

## 29. **Radishes and Sesame Seeds**

Preparation Time: 20 minutes
Cooking Time: 20-30 minutes
Servings: 4

**INGREDIENTS:**
- 20 radishes; halved
- 2 spring onions; chopped.
- 3 green onions; chopped.
- 2 tbsp. Olive oil
- 1 tbsp. Olive oil
- 3 tsp. Black sesame seeds
- Salt and black pepper to taste.

**DIRECTIONS:**
1. Take a bowl and mix all the ingredients and toss well.
2. Put the radishes in your air fryer's basket, cook at 400°f for 15 minutes, divide between plates and serve as a side dish

**NUTRITION:** Calories: 150; Fat: 4g; Fiber: 2g; Carbohydrates: 3g; Protein: 5g

## 30. **Curry Cabbage**

Preparation Time: 25 minutes
Cooking Time: 20-30 minutes
Servings: 4

**INGREDIENTS:**
30 oz. Green cabbage; shredded
3 tbsp. Coconut oil; melted
1 tbsp. Red curry paste
A pinch of salt and black pepper

**DIRECTIONS:**
1. In a pan that fits the air fryer, combine the cabbage with the rest of the ingredients, toss, introduce the pan in the machine and cook at 380°f for 20 minutes
2. Divide between plates and serve as a side dish.

**NUTRITION:** Calories: 180; Fat: 14g; Fiber: 4g; Carbohydrates: 6g; Protein: 8g

## 31. Firecracker Shrimp

Preparation time: 10 minutes
Cooking time: 8 minutes
Servings: 4
**INGREDIENTS:**
**For the shrimp**

- 1 pound (453.592g) raw shrimp, peeled and deveined
- Salt
- Pepper
- 1 egg
- ½ cup all-purpose flour
- ¾ cup panko bread crumbs
- Cooking oil
- For the firecracker sauce
- ⅓ cup sour cream
- 2 tablespoons sriracha
- ¼ cup sweet chili sauce

**DIRECTIONS:**

1. Season the shrimp with salt and pepper to taste. In a small bowl, beat the egg. In another small bowl, place the flour. In a third small bowl, add the panko bread crumbs.
2. Spray the air fryer oven basket with cooking oil. Dip the shrimp in the flour, then the egg, and then the bread crumbs. Place the shrimp in the air fryer basket. It is okay to stack them. Spray the shrimp with cooking oil.
3. Cook for 4 minutes. Open the air fryer oven and flip the shrimp. I recommend flipping individually instead of shaking to keep the breading intact. Cook for an additional 4 minutes or until crisp.
4. While the shrimp is cooking, make the firecracker sauce: in a small bowl, combine the sour cream, sriracha, and sweet chili sauce. Mix well. Serve with the shrimp.

**NUTRITION:** Calories: 266; Carbohydrates: 23g; Fat: 6g; Protein: 27g; Fiber:1g

## 32. Crispy Cheesy Fish Fingers

Preparation time: 10 minutes
Cooking time: 20 minutes
Servings: 4
**INGREDIENTS:**

- Large cod fish filet, approximately 6-8 ounces, fresh or frozen and thawed, cut into 1 ½-inch strips
- 2 raw eggs
- ½ cup of breadcrumbs (we like panko, but any brand or home recipe will do)
- 2 tablespoons of shredded or powdered parmesan cheese
- 1 tablespoons of shredded cheddar cheese
- Pinch of salt and pepper

**DIRECTIONS:**

1. Cover the basket of the air fryer oven with a lining of tin foil, leaving the edges uncovered to allow air to circulate through the basket.
2. Preheat the air fryer oven to 350 degrees.
3. In a large mixing bowl, beat the eggs until fluffy and until the yolks and whites are fully combined.

4. Dunk all the fish strips in the beaten eggs, fully submerging.
5. In a separate mixing bowl, combine the bread crumbs with the parmesan, cheddar, and salt and pepper, until evenly mixed.
6. One by one, coat the egg-covered fish strips in the mixed dry ingredients so that they're fully covered, and place on the foil-lined air fryer basket.
7. Set the air fryer oven timer to 20 minutes.
8. Halfway through the cooking time, shake the handle of the air fryer so that the breaded fish jostles inside and fry coverage is even.
9. After 20 minutes, when the fryer shuts off, the fish strips will be perfectly cooked and their breaded crust golden-brown and delicious! Using tongs, remove from the air fryer and set on a serving dish to cool.

**NUTRITION:** Calories: 124, Protein: 6.86g, Fat: 5.93g, Carbohydrates: 12.26g

## 33. Salmon Croquettes

Preparation time: 5 minutes
Cooking time: 10 minutes
Servings: 6-8
**INGREDIENTS:**

- Panko breadcrumbs
- Almond flour
- 2 egg whites
- 2 tbsp. Chopped chives
- 2 tbsp. Minced garlic cloves
- ½ c. Chopped onion
- 2/3 c. Grated carrots
- 1 pound (453.592g) chopped salmon fillet

**DIRECTIONS:**

1. Mix together all ingredients minus breadcrumbs, flour, and egg whites.
2. Shape mixture into balls. Then coat them in flour, then egg, and then breadcrumbs. Drizzle with olive oil.
3. Pour the coated salmon balls into the oven rack/basket. Place the rack on the middle-shelf of the air fryer oven. Set temperature to 350°f, and set time to 6 minutes. Shake and cook an additional 4 minutes until golden in color.

**NUTRITION:** Calories: 503; Carbohydrates: 61g; Fat: 9g; Protein: 5g;

## 34. Fried Calamari

Preparation time: 8 minutes
Cooking time: 7 minutes
Servings: 6-8
**INGREDIENTS:**

- ½ tsp. Salt
- ½ tsp. Old bay seasoning
- 1/3 c. Plain cornmeal
- ½ c. Semolina flour
- ½ c. Almond flour
- 5-6 c. Olive oil
- 1 ½ pounds (680.389g) baby squid

**DIRECTIONS:**

1. Rinse squid in cold water and slice tentacles, keeping just ¼-inch of the hood in one piece.

2. Combine 1-2 pinches of pepper, salt, old bay seasoning, cornmeal, and both flours together. Dredge squid pieces into flour mixture and place into the air fryer basket.
3. Spray liberally with olive oil. Cook 15 minutes at 345 degrees till coating turns a golden brown.

**NUTRITION:** Calories: 211; Carbohydrates: 55; Fat: 6g; Protein: 21g;

## 35. Soy and Ginger Shrimp

Preparation time: 8 minutes
Cooking time: 10 minutes
Servings: 4

**INGREDIENTS:**

- 2 tablespoons olive oil
- 2 tablespoons scallions, finely chopped
- 2 cloves garlic, chopped
- 1 teaspoon fresh ginger, grated
- 1 tablespoon dry white wine
- 1 tablespoon balsamic vinegar
- 1/4 cup soy sauce
- 1 tablespoon sugar
- 1 pound (453.592g) shrimp
- Salt and ground black pepper, to taste

**DIRECTIONS:**

1. To make the marinade, warm the oil in a saucepan; cook all ingredients, except the shrimp, salt, and black pepper. Now, let it cool.
2. Marinate the shrimp, covered, at least an hour, in the refrigerator.
3. After that, pour into the oven rack/basket. Place the rack on the middle-shelf of the air fryer oven. Set temperature to 350°f, and set time to 10 minutes. Bake the shrimp at 350 degrees f for 8 to 10 minutes (depending on the size), turning once or twice. Season prepared shrimp with salt and black pepper and serve.

**NUTRITION:** Calories: 233, Protein: 24.55g, Fat: 10.28g, Carbohydrates: 10.86g

## 36. Panko-crusted Tilapia

Preparation time: 5 minutes
Cooking time: 10 minutes
Servings: 3

**INGREDIENTS**

- 2 tsp. Italian seasoning
- 2 tsp. Lemon pepper
- 1/3 c. Panko breadcrumbs
- 1/3 c. Egg whites
- 1/3 c. Almond flour
- 3 tilapia fillets
- Olive oil

**DIRECTIONS:**

1. Place panko, egg whites, and flour into separate bowls. Mix lemon pepper and Italian seasoning in with breadcrumbs.
2. Pat tilapia fillets dry. Dredge in flour, then egg, then breadcrumb mixture.
3. Add to the air fryer basket and spray lightly with olive oil.
4. Cook 10-11 minutes at 400 degrees, making sure to flip halfway through cooking.

**NUTRITION:** Calories: 256; Fat: 9g; Protein: 39g;

## 37. Potato Crusted Salmon

Preparation time: 10 minutes
Cooking time: 15 minutes
Servings: 4
**INGREDIENTS:**

- 1 pound (453.592g) salmon, swordfish or arctic char fillets, 3/4 inch thick
- 1 egg white
- 2 tablespoons water
- 1/3 cup dry instant mashed potatoes
- 2 teaspoons cornstarch
- 1 teaspoon paprika
- 1 teaspoon lemon pepper seasoning

**DIRECTIONS:**

1. Remove and skin from the fish and cut it into 4 serving pieces mix together the egg white and water. Mix together all of the dry ingredients. Dip the filets into the egg white mixture then press into the potato mix to coat evenly.
2. Pour into the oven rack/basket. Place the rack on the middle-shelf of the air fryer oven. Set temperature to 360°f, and set time to 15 minutes, flip the filets halfway through.

**NUTRITION:** Calories: 176; Fat: 7g; Protein: 23g; Carbohydrates: 5g

## 38. Snapper Scampi

Preparation time: 5 minutes
Cooking time: 10 minutes
Servings: 4
**INGREDIENTS:**

- 4 (6-ounce) skinless snapper or arctic char fillets
- 1 tablespoon olive oil
- 3 tablespoons lemon juice, divided
- ½ teaspoon dried basil
- Pinch salt
- Freshly ground black pepper
- 2 tablespoons butter
- Cloves garlic, minced

**DIRECTIONS:**

1. Rub the fish fillets with olive oil and 1 tablespoon of the lemon juice. Sprinkle with the basil, salt, and pepper, and place in the air fryer oven basket.
2. Grill the fish for 7 to 8 minutes or until the fish just flakes when tested with a fork. Remove the fish from the basket and put on a serving plate. Cover to keep warm. In a 6-by-6-by-2-inch pan, combine the butter, remaining 2 tablespoons lemon juice, and garlic. Cook in the air fryer oven for 1 to 2 minutes or until the garlic is sizzling. Pour this mixture over the fish and serve.

**NUTRITION:** Calories: 265; Carbohydrates:1g; Fat: 11g; Protein:3 9g; Fiber: 0g

## 39. Thai Fish Cakes with Mango Relish

Preparation time: 5 minutes
Cooking time: 10 minutes
Servings: 4

**INGREDIENTS:**

- 1 lb. (453.592g) white fish fillets
- 3 tbsps. ground coconut
- 1 ripened mango
- ½ tsps. chili paste
- 2 Tbsps. fresh parsley
- 1 green onion
- 1 lime
- 1 tsp salt
- 1 egg

**DIRECTIONS:**

1. To make the relish, peel and dice the mango into cubes. Combine with a half teaspoon of chili paste, a tablespoon of parsley, and the zest and juice of half a lime.
2. In a food processor, pulse the fish until it forms a smooth texture. Place into a bowl and add the salt, egg, chopped green onion, parsley, two tablespoons of the coconut, and the remainder of the chili paste and lime zest and juice. Combine well
3. Portion the mixture into 10 equal balls and flatten them into small patties. Pour the reserved tablespoon of coconut onto a dish and roll the patties over to coat.
4. Preheat the air fryer oven to 390 degrees
5. Place the fish cakes into the air fryer oven and cook for 8 minutes. They should be crisp and lightly browned when ready
6. Serve hot with mango relish

**NUTRITION:** Calories: 169, Protein: 22.41g, Fat: 5.36g, Carbohydrates: 6.91g

## 40. Tuna Stuffed Potatoes

Preparation time: 5 minutes
Cooking time: 30 minutes
Servings: 4

**INGREDIENTS:**

- 4 starchy potatoes
- ½ tablespoon olive oil
- 1 (6-ounce) can tuna, drained
- 2 tablespoons plain Greek yogurt
- 1 teaspoon red chili powder
- Salt and freshly ground black pepper, to taste
- 1 scallion, chopped and divided
- 1 tablespoon capers

**DIRECTIONS:**

1. In a large bowl of water, soak the potatoes for about 30 minutes. Drain well and pat dry with paper towel.
2. Preheat the air fryer to 355 degrees f. Place the potatoes in a fryer basket.
3. Cook for about 30 minutes.
4. Meanwhile in a bowl, add tuna, yogurt, red chili powder, salt, black pepper and half of scallion and with a potato masher, mash the mixture completely.

5. Remove the potatoes from the air fryer oven and place onto a smooth surface.
6. Carefully, cut each potato from top side lengthwise.
7. With your fingers, press the open side of potato halves slightly. Stuff the potato open portion with tuna mixture evenly.
8. Sprinkle with the capers and remaining scallion. Serve immediately.

**NUTRITION:** Calories: 795, Protein: 109.77g Fat: 5.4g Carbohydrates: 43g

# Poultry

## 41. Chicken Stir-Fry

Preparation Time: 10 minutes
Cooking Time: 20 minutes
Servings: 2
**INGREDIENTS:**

- 1 (6-oz. chicken breast; cut into 1-inch cubes
- ½ medium red bell pepper; seeded and chopped
- ½ medium zucchini; chopped
- ¼ medium red onion; peeled and sliced
- 1 tbsp. coconut oil
- ½ tsp. garlic powder.
- 1 tsp. dried oregano.
- ¼ tsp. dried thyme

**DIRECTIONS:**

1. Place all ingredients into a large mixing bowl and toss until the coconut oil coats the meat and vegetables. Pour the contents of the bowl into the air fryer basket
2. Adjust the temperature to 375 Degrees F and set the timer for 15 minutes. Shake the fryer basket halfway through the cooking time to redistribute the food. Serve immediately.

**NUTRITION:** Calories: 186; Protein: 20.4g; Fiber: 1.7g; Fat: 8.0g; Carbohydrates: 5.6g

## 42. Chicken Pizza Crust

Preparation Time: 10 minutes
Cooking Time: 25 minutes
Servings: 4
**INGREDIENTS:**

- 1 lb. ground chicken thigh meat
- ½ cup shredded mozzarella
- ¼ cup grated Parmesan cheese.

**DIRECTIONS:**

1. Take a large bowl, mix all ingredients. Separate into four even parts.
2. Cut out four (6-inchcircles of parchment and press each portion of the chicken mixture out onto one of the circles. Place into the air fryer basket, working in batches as needed
3. Adjust the temperature to 375 Degrees F and set the timer for 25 minutes. Flip the crust halfway through the cooking time
4. Once fully cooked, you may top it with cheese and your favorite toppings and cook 5 additional minutes. Or, you may place crust into refrigerator or freezer and top when ready to eat.

**NUTRITION:** Calories: 230; Protein: 24.7g; Fiber: 0.0g; Fat: 12.8g; Carbohydrates: 1.2g

## 43. Spiced Chicken Breasts

Preparation Time: 15 minutes
Cooking Time: 10 minutes
Servings: 4
**INGREDIENTS:**

- 4 chicken breasts, skinless and boneless
- 1 tbsp. parsley; chopped
- 1 tsp. smoked paprika

- 1 tsp. garlic powder
- 1 tsp. chili powder
- A drizzle of olive oil
- A pinch of salt and black pepper

**DIRECTIONS:**
1. Season chicken with salt and pepper and rub it with the oil and all the other ingredients except the parsley
2. Put the chicken breasts in your air fryer's basket and cook at 350°F for 10 minutes on each side
3. Divide between plates, sprinkle the parsley on top and serve

**NUTRITION:** Calories: 222; Fat: 11g; Fiber: 4g; Carbohydrates: 6g; Protein: 12g

## 44. Spiced Duck Legs

Preparation Time: 5 minutes
Cooking Time: 25 minutes
Servings: 4

**INGREDIENTS:**
- 4 duck legs
- 2 garlic cloves; minced
- 2 tbsp. olive oil
- 1 tsp. five spice
- 1 tsp. hot chili powder
- A pinch of salt and black pepper

**DIRECTIONS:**
1. Take a bowl and mix the duck legs with all the other ingredients and rub them well.
2. Put the duck legs in your air fryer's basket and cook at 380°F for 25 minutes, flipping them halfway
3. Divide between plates and serve

**NUTRITION:** Calories: 287; Fat: 12g; Fiber: 4g; Carbohydrates: 6g; Protein: 17g

## 45. Nutmeg Chicken Thighs

Preparation Time: 15 minutes
Cooking Time: 20 minutes
Servings: 4

**INGREDIENTS:**
- 2 lb. chicken thighs
- 2 tbsp. olive oil
- ½ tsp. nutmeg, ground
- A pinch of salt and black pepper

**DIRECTIONS:**
1. Season the chicken thighs with salt and pepper and rub with the rest of the ingredients
2. Put the chicken thighs in air fryer's basket, cook at 360°F for 15 minutes on each side, divide between plates and serve.

**NUTRITION:** Calories: 271; Fat: 12g; Fiber: 4g; Carbohydrates: 6g; Protein: 13g

## 46. Creamy Chicken Wings

Preparation Time: 5 minutes
Cooking Time: 30 minutes
Servings: 4

**INGREDIENTS:**
- 2 lb. chicken wings

- ¼ cup parmesan, grated
- ½ cup heavy cream
- 3 garlic cloves; minced
- 3 tbsp. butter; melted
- ½ tsp. oregano; dried
- ½ tsp. basil; dried
- Salt and black pepper to taste.

**DIRECTIONS:**
1. In a baking dish that fits your air fryer, mix the chicken wings with all the ingredients except the parmesan and toss
2. Put the dish to your air fryer and cook at 380°F for 30 minutes. Sprinkle the cheese on top, leave the mix aside for 10 minutes, divide between plates and serve

**NUTRITION:** Calories: 270; Fat: 12g; Fiber: 3g; Carbohydrates: 6g; Protein: 17g

## 47. **Cheddar Turkey Bites**

Preparation Time: 5 minutes
Cooking Time: 20 minutes
Servings: 4

**INGREDIENTS:**
- 1 big turkey breast, skinless; boneless and cubed
- 1 tbsp. olive oil
- ¼ cup cheddar cheese, grated
- ¼ tsp. garlic powder
- Salt and black pepper to taste.

**DIRECTIONS:**
1. Rub the turkey cubes with the oil, season with salt, pepper and garlic powder and dredge in cheddar cheese.
2. Put the turkey bits in your air fryer's basket and cook at 380°F for 20 minutes. Divide between plates and serve with a side salad

**NUTRITION:** Calories: 240;Fat: 11g;Fiber: 2g;Carbohydrates: 5g;Protein: 12g

## 48. **Chicken Parmesan**

Preparation Time: 5 minutes
Cooking Time: 25 minutes
Servings: 4

**INGREDIENTS:**
- 2 (6-oz.boneless, skinless chicken breasts
- 1 oz. pork rinds, crushed
- ½ cup grated Parmesan cheese, divided.
- 1 cup low-carb, no-sugar-added pasta sauce.
- 1 cup shredded mozzarella cheese, divided.
- 4 tbsp. full-fat mayonnaise, divided.
- ½ tsp. garlic powder.
- ¼ tsp. dried oregano.
- ½ tsp. dried parsley.

**DIRECTIONS:**
1. Slice each chicken breast in half lengthwise and lb. out to 3/4-inch thickness. Sprinkle with garlic powder, oregano and parsley

2. Spread 1 tbsp. mayonnaise on top of each piece of chicken, then sprinkle ¼ cup mozzarella on each piece.
3. In a small bowl, mix the crushed pork rinds and Parmesan. Sprinkle the mixture on top of mozzarella
4. Pour sauce into 6-inch round baking pan and place chicken on top. Place pan into the air fryer basket. Adjust the temperature to 320 Degrees F and set the timer for 25 minutes
5. Cheese will be browned and internal temperature of the chicken will be at least 165 Degrees F when fully cooked. Serve warm.

**NUTRITION:** Calories: 393; Protein: 34.2g; Fiber: 2.1g; Fat: 22.8g; Carbohydrates: 6.8g

## 49. Lemon Pepper Drumsticks

Preparation Time: 5 minutes
Cooking Time: 25 minutes
Servings: 8 drumsticks
**INGREDIENTS:**

- 8 chicken drumsticks
- 1 tbsp. lemon pepper seasoning
- 4 tbsp. salted butter; melted.
- 2 tsp. baking powder.
- ½ tsp. garlic powder.

**DIRECTIONS:**
1. Sprinkle baking powder and garlic powder over drumsticks and rub into chicken skin. Place drumsticks into the air fryer basket.
2. Adjust the temperature to 375 Degrees F and set the timer for 25 minutes
3. Use tongs to turn drumsticks halfway through the cooking time. When skin is golden and internal temperature is at least 165 Degrees F, remove from fryer
4. Take a large bowl, mix butter and lemon pepper seasoning. Add drumsticks to the bowl and toss until coated. Serve warm.

**NUTRITION:** Calories: 532; Protein: 48.3g; Fiber: 0.0g; Fat: 32.3g; Carbohydrates: 1.2g

## 50. Mustard Turkey Bites

Preparation Time: 5 minutes
Cooking Time: 20 minutes
Servings: 4
**INGREDIENTS:**

- 1 big turkey breast, skinless; boneless and cubed
- 4 garlic cloves; minced
- 1 tbsp. mustard
- 1 ½ tbsp. olive oil
- Salt and black pepper to taste.

**DIRECTIONS:**
1. Take a bowl and mix the chicken with the garlic and the other ingredients and toss.
2. Put the turkey in your air fryer's basket, cook at 360°F for 20 minutes, divide between plates and serve with a side salad

**NUTRITION:** Calories: 240; Fat: 12g; Fiber: 4g; Carbohydrates: 6g; Protein: 15g

# Meat

## 51. Pork with Quinoa Salad

Preparation time: 10 minutes
Cooking time: 12 minutes
Serving: 4

**INGREDIENTS:**

- 2/3 lbs. (303.9g) Lean pork shoulder, cubed
- 1 teaspoon ground cumin
- ½ teaspoon cayenne pepper
- 1 teaspoon sweet smoked paprika
- 1 tablespoon olive oil
- 24 cherry tomatoes
- Salad:
- ½ cup quinoa, boiled
- ½ cup frozen pea
- 1 large carrot, grated
- Small pack coriander, chopped
- Small pack mint, chopped
- Juice 1 lemon
- 2 tablespoon olive oil

**DIRECTIONS:**

1. Toss pork with oil, paprika, pepper, and cumin in a bowl.
2. Alternatively, thread the pork on the skewers.
3. Place these pork skewers in the air fry basket.
4. Press "power button" of air fry oven and turn the dial to select the "air fryer" mode.
5. Press the time button and again turn the dial to set the cooking time to 10 minutes.
6. Now push the temp button and rotate the dial to set the temperature at 370 degrees f.
7. Once preheated, place the air fryer basket in the oven and close its lid.
8. Flip the skewers when cooked halfway through then resume cooking.
9. Meanwhile, sauté carrots and peas with olive oil in a pan for 2 minutes.
10. Stir in mint, lemon juice, coriander, and cooked quinoa.
11. Serve skewers with the couscous salad.

**NUTRITION:** Calories: 331 Fat: 20.1 g Carbohydrates: 20.1 g Fiber 0.9 g Protein 14.6 g

## 52. Rib Eye Steak

Preparation Time: 10 minutes
Cooking Time: 20 minutes
Servings: 2

**INGREDIENTS:**

- 1 pound ribeye steak
- Salt and black pepper, to taste
- ½ tablespoon olive oil

**For the rub:**

- 1 ½ tablespoon sweet paprika
- 1 tablespoon onion powder
- 1 tablespoon garlic powder

- ½ tablespoon brown sugar
- 1 tablespoon dried oregano
- ½ tablespoon ground cumin
- ½ tablespoon dried rosemary

**DIRECTIONS:**
1. Mix cumin, salt, pepper, rosemary, oregano, sugar, garlic powder, onion powder, and paprika in a bowl. Stir and rub steak with this mix.
2. Season steak with salt, pepper, and rub again with the oil.
3. Place in the air fryer and cook at 400F for 20 minutes, flipping once.
4. Slice and serve.

**NUTRITION:** Calories: 320 Fat: 8g Carbohydrates: 22g Protein: 21g

## 53. Provencal Pork

Preparation Time: 10 minutes
Cooking Time: 15 minutes
Servings: 2

**INGREDIENTS:**
- 1 red onion, sliced
- 1 yellow bell pepper, cut into strips
- 1 green bell pepper, cut into strips
- Salt and black pepper, to taste
- 2 teaspoons Provencal herbs
- ½ teaspoon mustard
- 1 tablespoon olive oil
- 7 ounces pork tenderloin

**DIRECTIONS:**
1. In a dish, mix salt, pepper, onion, green bell pepper, yellow bell pepper, half the oil, and herbs and toss well.
2. Season pork with mustard, salt, pepper, and rest of the oil. Toss well and add to vegetables.
3. Cook in the air fryer at 370F for 15 minutes.
4. Serve.

**NUTRITION:** Calories: 300 Fat: 8g Carbohydrates: 21g Protein: 23g

## 54. Lamb with Brussels Sprouts

Preparation Time: 10 minutes
Cooking Time: 1 hour and 10 minutes
Servings: 2

**INGREDIENTS:**
- 1 pound leg of lamb, scored
- 1 tablespoon olive oil
- ½ tablespoon rosemary, chopped
- ½ tablespoon lemon thyme, chopped
- 1 clove garlic, minced
- ¾ pound brussels sprouts, trimmed
- ½ tablespoon butter, melted
- ¼ cup sour cream
- Salt and black pepper, to taste

**DIRECTIONS:**

1. Season the leg of lamb with rosemary, thyme, salt, and pepper. Brush with oil, and place in the air fryer basket.
2. Cook at 300F for 1 hour. Transfer to a plate and keep warm.
3. In a pan, mix brussels sprouts with sour cream, butter, garlic, salt, and pepper. Mix well and cook at 400F for 10 minutes.
4. Divide lamb on plates, add Brussels sprouts on the side and serve.

**NUTRITION:** Calories: 440 Fat: 23g Carbohydrates: 2g Protein: 49g

## 55. Zesty Pork Skewers

Preparation time: 10 minutes
Cooking time: 20 minutes
Servings: 4

**INGREDIENTS:**

- 2 teaspoons ground cumin
- 2 teaspoons ground coriander
- 1 onion, cut into pieces
- 1/4 teaspoon ground cinnamon
- 1/8 teaspoon ground smoked paprika
- 2 teaspoons orange zest
- 1/2 yellow bell pepper, sliced into squares
- 1/2 teaspoon salt
- 1/2 teaspoon black pepper
- 1 tablespoon lemon juice
- 2 teaspoons olive oil
- 1 1/2 lbs. (680.389g) Pork, cubed

**DIRECTIONS:**

1. Toss pork with the rest of the skewer's ingredients in a bowl.
2. Thread the pork and veggies on the skewers alternately.
3. Place these pork skewers in the air fry basket.
4. Press "power button" of air fry oven and turn the dial to select the "air fryer" mode.
5. Press the time button and again turn the dial to set the cooking time to 20 minutes.
6. Now push the temp button and rotate the dial to set the temperature at 370 degrees f.
7. Once preheated, place the air fryer basket in the oven and close its lid.
8. Flip the skewers when cooked halfway through then resume cooking.
9. Serve warm.

**NUTRITION:** Calories: 327 Fat: 3.5 g Carbohydrates: 13.6 g  Fiber 0.4 g Protein 24.5 g

## 56. Beef Strips with Vegetables

Preparation Time: 10 minutes
Cooking Time: 22 minutes
Servings: 2

**INGREDIENTS:**

- 2 beef steaks, cut into strips
- Salt and black pepper, to taste
- 7 ounces of snow peas
- 8 ounces white mushrooms, halved
- 1 yellow onion, cut into rings

- 2 tablespoons soy sauce
- 1 teaspoon olive oil

**DIRECTIONS:**

1. In a bowl, mix soy sauce and olive oil, and whisk. Add beef strips and coat.
2. In another bowl, mix mushrooms, onion, snow peas with salt, pepper, and oil. Toss well.
3. Place in pan and cook in the air fryer at 350F for 16 minutes.
4. Add beef strips to the pan as well and cook at 400F for 6 minutes more.
5. Serve.

**NUTRITION:** Calories: 235 Fat: 8g Carbohydrates: 22g Protein: 24g

## 57. **Pork Garlic Skewers**

Preparation time: 10 minutes
Cooking time: 20 minutes
Servings: 4

**INGREDIENTS:**

- 1 lb. (453.592g) Pork, boned and diced
- 1 lemon, juiced and chopped
- 3 tablespoon olive oil
- 20 garlic cloves, chopped
- 1 handful rosemary, chopped
- 3 green peppers, cubed
- 2 red onions, cut into wedges

**DIRECTIONS:**

1. Toss the pork with the rest of the skewer's ingredients in a bowl.
2. Thread the pork, peppers, garlic, and onion on the skewers, alternately.
3. Place these pork skewers in the air fry basket.
4. Press "power button" of air fry oven and turn the dial to select the "air fryer" mode.
5. Press the time button and again turn the dial to set the cooking time to 20 minutes.
6. Now push the temp button and rotate the dial to set the temperature at 370 degrees f.
7. Once preheated, place the air fryer basket in the oven and close its lid.
8. Flip the skewers when cooked halfway through then resume cooking.
9. Serve warm.

**NUTRITION:** Calories: 472 Fat: 11.1 g Carbohydrates: 19.9 g  Fiber 0.2 g Protein 13.5 g

## 58. **Garlic Lamb Chops**

Preparation Time: 10 minutes
Cooking Time: 10 minutes
Servings: 2

**INGREDIENTS:**

- 1 ½ tablespoon olive oil
- 4 lamb chops
- Salt and black pepper, to taste
- 2 cloves garlic, minced
- ½ tablespoons oregano, chopped
- ½ tablespoon coriander, chopped

**DIRECTIONS:**

1. In a bowl, mix oregano with garlic, oil, salt, pepper, and lamb chops and coat well.
2. Cook in the air fryer at 400F for 10 minutes.
3. Serve.

**NUTRITION:** Calories: 231 Fat: 7g Carbohydrates: 14g Protein: 23g

## 59. Pork Sausage with Yogurt Dip

Preparation time: 10 minutes
Cooking time: 10 minutes
Servings: 8

**INGREDIENTS:**

- 2 tablespoon cumin seed
- 2 tablespoon coriander seed
- 2 tablespoon fennel seed
- 1 tablespoon paprika
- 4 garlic cloves, minced
- ½ teaspoon ground cinnamon
- 1 ½ lb. (680.389g) Lean minced pork

**For the yogurt**

- 3 zucchinis, grated
- 2 teaspoon cumin seed, toasted
- 9 0z. Greek yogurt
- Small handful chopped the coriander
- A small handful of chopped mint

**DIRECTIONS:**

1. Blend all the spices and seeds with garlic and cinnamon in a blender.
2. Add this spice paste to the minced pork then mix well.
3. Make 8 sausages and thread each on the skewers.
4. Place these pork skewers in the air fry basket.
5. Press "power button" of air fry oven and turn the dial to select the "air fryer" mode.
6. Press the time button and again turn the dial to set the cooking time to 10 minutes.
7. Now push the temp button and rotate the dial to set the temperature at 370 degrees f.
8. Once preheated, place the air fryer basket in the oven and close its lid.
9. Flip the skewers when cooked halfway through then resume cooking.
10. Prepare the yogurt ingredients in a bowl.
11. Serve skewers with the yogurt mixture.

**NUTRITION:** Calories: 341 Fat: 20.5 g Carbohydrates: 20.3 g  Fiber 4.3 g Protein 49 g

## 60. Aleppo Pork Kebabs

Preparation time: 10 minutes
Cooking time:  16 minutes
Servings: 6

**INGREDIENTS:**

- Pork kebabs
- 1 lb. (453.592g) Ground pork
- 1/2 an onion, finely diced
- 3 garlic cloves, finely minced
- 2 teaspoons cumin
- 2 teaspoons coriander
- 2 teaspoons sumac
- 1 teaspoon Aleppo chili flakes
- 1 ½ teaspoons salt

- 2 tablespoons chopped mint

**DIRECTIONS:**
1. Toss pork with the rest of the kebob ingredients in a bowl.
2. Make 6 sausages out of this mince and thread them on the skewers.
3. Place these pork skewers in the air fry basket.
4. Press "power button" of air fry oven and turn the dial to select the "air fryer" mode.
5. Press the time button and again turn the dial to set the cooking time to 16 minutes.
6. Now push the temp button and rotate the dial to set the temperature at 370 degrees f.
7. Once preheated, place the air fryer basket in the oven and close its lid.
8. Flip the skewers when cooked halfway through then resume cooking.
9. Serve the skewers with yogurt sauce.

**NUTRITION:** Calories: 353 Fat: 7.5 g Carbohydrates: 10.4 g  Fiber 0.2 g Protein 13.1 g

# Vegetables

## 61. Mediterranean Vegetables

Preparation time: 5 minutes
Cooking time: 20 minutes
Servings: 4

**INGREDIENTS:**

- ¼ cup cherry tomatoes
- 1 large courgette
- 1 green pepper, chopped
- 1 large parsnip, sliced
- 1 medium carrot, sliced
- 1 teaspoon mixed herbs
- 2 tablespoons honey
- 1 teaspoon mustard
- 2 teaspoons garlic puree
- 6 tablespoons olive oil
- Salt and pepper

**DIRECTIONS:**

1. Add courgettes, green pepper, parsnip, carrot, and cherry tomatoes to the air fryer.
2. Pour three tablespoons of olive oil over veggies and cook for 15 minutes at 180 degrees F.
3. Add and mix the remaining ingredients in a bowl.
4. Add vegetables to the prepared marinade.
5. Return the veggies to the air fryer basket for 5 minutes at 200 degrees F.
6. Serve.

**NUTRITION:** Calories: 372 Fat: 11.1 g Carbohydrates: 0.9 g Fiber: 0.2 g Protein: 63.5 g

## 62. Mushroom, Onion and Feta Frittata

Preparation time: 5 minutes
Cooking Time: 30 minutes
Servings: 4

**INGREDIENTS:**

- 4 cups button mushrooms
- 1 red onion
- 2 tablespoons olive oil
- 6 tablespoons feta cheese, crumbled
- Pinch of salt
- 6 eggs
- Cooking spray

**DIRECTIONS:**

1. Peel and slice the red onion into ¼ inch thin slices. Clean the button mushrooms, then cut them into ¼ inch thin slices. Add olive oil to pan and sauté mushrooms over medium heat until tender. Remove from heat and pan so that they can cool. Preheat your air fryer to 330°Fahrenheit. Add cracked eggs into a bowl, and whisk them, adding a pinch of salt. Coat an 8-inch heat resistant baking dish with cooking spray. Add the eggs into the baking dish, then onion and mushroom mixture, and then add feta cheese. Place the baking dish into air fryer for 30-minutes and serve warm.

**NUTRITION:** Calories: 246 Total Fat: 12.3g Carbohydrates: 9.2g Protein: 10.3g

## 63. Cauliflower pizza crust

Preparation Time: 26 minutes
Cooking Time: 20 minutes
Servings: 2

**INGREDIENTS:**

- 1 (12-oz.) Steamer bag cauliflower
- 1 large egg.
- ½ cup shredded sharp cheddar cheese.
- 2 tbsp. Blanched finely ground almond flour
- 1 tsp. Italian blend seasoning

**DIRECTIONS:**

1. Cook cauliflower according to package instructions. Remove from bag and place into cheesecloth or paper towel to remove excess water. Place cauliflower into a large bowl.
2. Add cheese, egg, almond flour and Italian seasoning to the bowl and mix well
3. Cut a piece of parchment to fit your air fryer basket. Press cauliflower into 6-inch round circle. Place into the air fryer basket. Adjust the temperature to 360 degrees f and set the timer for 11 minutes. After 7 minutes, flip the pizza crust
4. Add preferred toppings to pizza. Place back into air fryer basket and cook an additional 4 minutes or until fully cooked and golden. Serve immediately.

**NUTRITION:** Calories: 230 Protein: 14.9g Fiber: 4.7g Fat: 14.2g Carbohydrates: 10.0g

## 64. Olives and artichokes

Preparation Time: 20 minutes
Cooking Time: 15 minutes
Servings: 4

**INGREDIENTS:**

- 14 oz. Canned artichoke hearts, drained
- ½ cup tomato sauce
- 2 cups black olives, pitted
- 3 garlic cloves; minced
- 1 tbsp. Olive oil
- 1 tsp. Garlic powder

**DIRECTIONS:**

1. In a pan that fits your air fryer, mix the olives with the artichokes and the other ingredients, toss, put the pan in the fryer and cook at 350°f for 15 minutes
2. Divide the mix between plates and serve.

**NUTRITION:** Calories: 180 Fat: 4g Fiber: 3g Carbohydrates: 5g Protein: 6g

## 65. Lemon asparagus

Preparation Time: 17 minutes
Cooking Time: 12 minutes
Servings: 4

**INGREDIENTS:**

- 1 lb. Asparagus, trimmed
- 3 garlic cloves; minced
- 3 tbsp. Parmesan, grated

- 2 tbsp. Olive oil
- Juice of 1 lemon
- A pinch of salt and black pepper

**DIRECTIONS:**
1. Take a bowl and mix the asparagus with the rest of the ingredients and toss.
2. Put the asparagus in your air fryer's basket and cook at 390°f for 12 minutes. Divide between plates and serve

**NUTRITION:** Calories: 175 Fat: 5g Fiber: 2g Carbohydrates: 4g Protein: 8g

## 66. Savory cabbage and tomatoes

Preparation Time: 20 minutes
Cooking Time: 15 minutes
Servings: 4

**INGREDIENTS:**
- 2 spring onions; chopped.
- 1 savoy cabbage, shredded
- 1 tbsp. Parsley; chopped.
- 2 tbsp. Tomato sauce
- Salt and black pepper to taste.

**DIRECTIONS:**
1. In a pan that fits your air fryer, mix the cabbage the rest of the ingredients except the parsley, toss, put the pan in the fryer and cook at 360°f for 15 minutes
2. Divide between plates and serve with parsley sprinkled on top.

**NUTRITION:** Calories: 163 Fat: 4g Fiber: 3g Carbohydrates: 6g Protein: 7g

## 67. Pecan brownies

Preparation Time: 30 minutes
Cooking Time: 20 minutes
Servings: 6

**INGREDIENTS:**
- ¼ cup chopped pecans
- ¼ cup low carb
- Sugar: -free chocolate chips.
- ¼ cup unsalted butter; softened.
- 1 large egg.
- ½ cup blanched finely ground almond flour.
- ½ cup powdered erythritol
- 2 tbsp. Unsweetened cocoa powder
- ½ tsp. Baking powder.

**DIRECTIONS:**
1. Take a large bowl, mix almond flour, erythritol, cocoa powder and baking powder. Stir in butter and egg.
2. Fold in pecans and chocolate chips. Scoop mixture into 6-inch round baking pan. Place pan into the air fryer basket.
3. Adjust the temperature to 300 degrees f and set the timer for 20 minutes. When fully cooked a toothpick inserted in center will come out clean. Allow 20 minutes to fully cool and firm up.

**NUTRITION:** Calories: 215 Protein: 4.2g Fiber: 2.8g Fat: 18.9g Carbohydrates: 21.8g

## 68. Cheesy endives

Preparation Time: 20 minutes
Cooking Time: 15 minutes
Servings: 4

**INGREDIENTS:**

- 4 endives, trimmed
- ¼ cup goat cheese, crumbled
- 1 tbsp. Lemon juice
- 2 tbsp. Chives; chopped.
- 2 tbsp. Olive oil
- 1 tsp. Lemon zest, grated
- A pinch of salt and black pepper

**DIRECTIONS:**

1. Take a bowl and mix the endives with the other ingredients except the cheese and chives and toss well.
2. Put the endives in your air fryer's basket and cook at 380°f for 15 minutes
3. Divide the corn between plates and serve with cheese and chives sprinkled on top.

**NUTRITION:** Calories: 140 Fat: 4g Fiber: 3g Carbohydrates: 5g Protein: 7g

## 69. Cauliflower steak

Preparation Time: 12 minutes
Cooking Time: 7 minutes
Servings: 4

**INGREDIENTS:**

- 1 medium head cauliflower
- ¼ cup blue cheese crumbles
- ¼ cup hot sauce
- ¼ cup full-fat ranch dressing
- 2 tbsp. Salted butter; melted.

**DIRECTIONS:**

1. Remove cauliflower leaves. Slice the head in ½-inch-thick slices.
2. In a small bowl, mix hot sauce and butter. Brush the mixture over the cauliflower.
3. Place each cauliflower steak into the air fryer, working in batches if necessary. Adjust the temperature to 400 degrees f and set the timer for 7 minutes
4. When cooked, edges will begin turning dark and caramelized. To serve, sprinkle steaks with crumbled blue cheese. Drizzle with ranch dressing.

**NUTRITION:** Calories: 122 Protein: 4.9g Fiber: 3.0g Fat: 8.4g Carbohydrates: 7.7g

## 70. Parmesan Broccoli and Asparagus

Preparation Time: 20 minutes
Cooking Time: 15 minutes
Servings: 4

**INGREDIENTS:**

- ½ lb. asparagus, trimmed
- 1 broccoli head, florets separated
- Juice of 1 lime
- 3 tbsp. parmesan, grated
- 2 tbsp. olive oil

- Salt and black pepper to taste.

**DIRECTIONS:**

1. Take a bowl and mix the asparagus with the broccoli and all the other ingredients except the parmesan, toss, transfer to your air fryer's basket and cook at 400°F for 15 minutes
2. Divide between plates, sprinkle the parmesan on top and serve.

**NUTRITION:** Calories: 172;Fat: 5g; Fiber: 2g; Carbohydrates: 4g; Protein: 9g

# Soups and Stews

## 71. White Bean and Swiss Chard Stew

Preparation Time: 10-20 minutes
Cooking Time: 15 minutes
Servings: 5

**INGREDIENTS:**

- 2 cups cooked great northern beans
- 2 carrots, sliced, with thicker end cut into half-moons
- 1 small bunch Swiss chard leaves, chopped
- 1 celery stalk, sliced
- 1/2 onion; cut into large dice
- 2 or 3 garlic cloves; minced
- 3 tomatoes, chopped
- 1 tbsp. olive oil
- ¼ to ½ tsp. red pepper flakes
- 1/2 tsp. dried rosemary
- 1/2 tsp. dried oregano
- 1/4 tsp. dried basil
- 1/2 tsp. salt or as your liking
- Pinch freshly ground black pepper; or more as needed
- Nutritional yeast, for sprinkling; optional

**DIRECTIONS:**

1. Select the "Sauté" Low mode on your instant pot. When the display reads "Hot," add the oil and heat until it shimmers.
2. Add the carrots, celery and onion. Cook for 2 to 3 minutes, stirring occasionally. Add the garlic and cook for 30 seconds more. Turn off the Instant Pot
3. Stir in the tomatoes, red pepper flakes, rosemary; oregano, basil, salt, pepper and beans. Lock the lid and turn the steam release handle to Sealing. Using the Manual function, set the cooker to High Pressure for 4 minutes.
4. After completing the cooking time, quick release the pressure.
5. Remove the lid carefully and stir in the Swiss chard. Let wilt for 2 to 3 minutes
6. Taste and season with salt and pepper, as needed and sprinkle the nutritional yeast over individual servings.

**NUTRITION:** Calories: 230 Fat: 5 g Protein:1 g

## 72. Surprising Sweet Potato Stew

Preparation Time: 10-20 minutes
Cooking Time: 40 minutes
Servings: 4

**INGREDIENTS:**

- 1 sweet potato, cubed
- 1 big onion; chopped.
- 1/2 cup red lentils
- 3 garlic cloves; chopped.
- 1 celery stalk; chopped.
- 2 cups veggie stock

- 1/4 cup raisins
- 2 carrots; chopped
- 1 cup green lentils
- 14 oz. canned tomatoes; chopped.
- Salt and black pepper to the taste

**For the spice blend:**

- 1/2 tsp. cinnamon
- 1/4 tsp. ginger, grated
- 1 tsp. cumin
- 1 tsp. paprika
- 2 tsp. coriander
- 1 tsp. turmeric
- A pinch of cloves
- A pinch of chili flakes

**DIRECTIONS:**

1. Set your instant pot on Sauté mode; add onions and brown them for 2 minutes adding some of the stock from time to time
2. Add garlic, stir and cook for 1 minute
3. Add carrots, raisins, celery, and sweet potatoes, stir and cook for 1 minute.
4. Add red and green lentils, stock, tomatoes, salt, pepper, turmeric, cinnamon, paprika, cumin, coriander, ginger, cloves and chili flakes; then stir well. seal the instant pot lid and cook at High for 15 minutes.
5. Release the pressure naturally for 15 minutes, then release remaining pressure by turning the valve to 'Venting', carefully open the lid; stir stew one more time, add more salt and pepper if needed, ladle into bowls and serve

**NUTRITION:** Calories: 230 Fat: 5 g Protein:1 g

## 73. Zuppa Toscana Delight

Preparation Time: 10-20 minutes
Cooking Time: 40 minutes
Servings: 8

**INGREDIENTS:**

- 1 lb. chicken sausage, ground.
- 6 bacon slices; chopped
- 12 oz. evaporated milk
- 1 cup parmesan, shredded.
- 2 cup spinach; chopped
- 3 potatoes, cubed
- 3 tbsp. cornstarch
- 3 garlic cloves; minced.
- 1 cup yellow onion; chopped.
- 1 tbsp. butter
- 40 oz. chicken stock
- Salt and black pepper to the taste
- A pinch of red pepper flakes

**DIRECTIONS:**

1. Set your instant pot on Sauté mode; add bacon; then stir well. cook until it's crispy and transfer to a plate
2. Add sausage to the pot; then stir well. cook until it browns on all sides and also transfer to a plate
3. Add butter to the pot and melt it
4. Add onion, stir and cook for 5 minutes
5. Add garlic, stir and cook for 1 minute
6. Add 1/3 of the stock, salt, pepper and pepper flakes and stir.
7. Place potatoes in the steamer basket of the pot, seal the instant pot lid and cook at High for 4 minutes.
8. Release the pressure naturally for 15 minutes, then release remaining pressure by turning the valve to 'Venting', carefully open the lid and transfer potatoes to a bowl.
9. Add the rest of the stock to the pot, cornstarch mixed with some evaporated milk and the milk, stir and set the pot on Simmer mode.
10. Add parmesan, sausage, bacon, potatoes, spinach, more salt and pepper if needed; then stir well. divide into bowls and serve

**NUTRITION:** Calories: 150 Fat: 5 g Protein: 1 g

## 74. Bacon and Broccoli Soup

Preparation Time: 10-20 minutes
Cooking Time: 30 minutes
Servings: 6

**INGREDIENTS:**

- 4 bacon slices; chopped
- 2 small broccoli heads; chopped.
- 1 tbsp. parmesan, grated
- 1 leek; chopped
- 1 celery rib; chopped
- 1-quart veggie stock
- 1 tsp. olive oil
- 2 cups spinach; chopped
- 4 tbsp. basmati rice
- Salt and black pepper to the taste

**DIRECTIONS:**

1. Set your instant pot on Sauté mode; add oil and bacon, cook until it's crispy, transfer to a plate and leave aside
2. Add broccoli, leek, celery, spinach, rice, salt, pepper and veggie stock; then stir well. seal the instant pot lid and cook at High for 6 minutes
3. Release the pressure naturally for 15 minutes, then release remaining pressure by turning the valve to 'Venting', carefully open the lid; add more salt and pepper if needed, add bacon, divide into soup bowls and serve with parmesan on top.

**NUTRITION:** Calories: 160 Fat: 4 g Protein: 1 g

## 75. Chicken Noodle Soup

Preparation Time: 10-20 minutes
Cooking Time: 35 minutes
Servings: 6

**INGREDIENTS:**

- 2 cups chicken, already cooked and shredded.

- 4 carrots, sliced
- 1 yellow onion; chopped
- 1 tbsp. butter
- 6 cups chicken stock
- 1 celery rib; chopped
- Salt and black pepper to the taste
- Egg noodles, already cooked

**DIRECTIONS:**
1. Set your instant pot on Sauté mode; add butter and heat it up.
2. Add onion, stir and cook 2 minutes
3. Add celery and carrots, stir and cook 5 minutes
4. Add chicken, stock; then stir well. close the lid and cook at High for 5 minutes
5. Release the pressure naturally for 15 minutes, then release remaining pressure by turning the valve to 'Venting', carefully open the lid; add salt and pepper to the taste and stir
6. Divide noodles into soup bowls, add soup over them and serve.

**NUTRITION:** Calories: 130 Fat: 4 g Protein:3 g

## 76. **Beef and Mushroom Stew**

Preparation Time: 10-20 minutes
Cooking Time: 45 minutes
Servings: 6

**INGREDIENTS:**
- 2 lb. beef chuck, cubed
- 1 celery stalk; chopped.
- 1 oz. dried porcini mushrooms; chopped.
- 2 carrots; chopped
- 2 tbsp. butter
- 1/2 cup red wine
- 1 cup beef stock
- 2 tbsp. flour
- 1 tbsp. olive oil
- 1 red onion; chopped
- 1 tsp. rosemary; chopped
- Salt and black pepper to the taste

**DIRECTIONS:**
1. Set your instant pot on Sauté mode; add oil and beef, stir and brown for 5 minutes
2. Add onion, celery, rosemary, salt, pepper, wine and stock and stir
3. Add carrots and mushrooms, close the lid and cook at High for 15 minutes.
4. Release the pressure naturally for 15 minutes, then release remaining pressure by turning the valve to 'Venting', open the instant pot lid and set it on Simmer mode
5. Meanwhile, heat up a pan over medium high heat, add butter and melt it
6. Add flour and 6 tablespoon of cooking liquid from the stew and stir well
7. Pour this over stew; then stir well. cook for 5 minutes, divide into bowls and serve

**NUTRITION:** Calories: 160 Fat: 4 g Protein: 1 g

## 77. Chicken Chili Soup

Preparation Time: 10-20 minutes
Cooking Time: 50 minutes
Servings: 4

**INGREDIENTS:**

- 1 lb. chicken breast, skinless and boneless
- 30 oz. canned cannellini beans, drained
- 4 garlic cloves; minced.
- 2 tsp. oregano, dried
- 1 tsp. cumin
- 1 white onion; chopped.
- 2 tbsp. olive oil
- 1/2 tsp. red pepper flakes, crushed.
- 3 cups chicken stock
- 1 jalapeno pepper; chopped.
- Salt and black pepper to the taste
- Cilantro; chopped for serving
- Tortilla chips, for serving
- Lime wedges for serving

**DIRECTIONS:**

1. Set your instant pot on Sauté mode; add oil and heat it up.
2. Add jalapeno and onion, stir and cook for 3 minutes
3. Add garlic, stir and cook for 1 minute.
4. Add oregano, cumin, pepper flakes, stock, chicken, beans, salt and pepper; then stir well. seal the instant pot lid and cook on Low for 30 minutes.
5. Release the pressure naturally for 15 minutes, then release remaining pressure by turning the valve to 'Venting', carefully open the lid; shred meat with 2 forks, add more salt and pepper, stir and divide into soup bowls
6. Serve with cilantro on top and with tortilla chips and lime wedges on the side

**NUTRITION:** Calories: 186 Fat: 4 g Protein: 1 g

## 78. Minestrone Soup

Preparation Time: 10-20 minutes
Cooking Time: 35 minutes
Servings: 8

**INGREDIENTS:**

- 29 oz. canned chicken stock
- 15 oz. canned kidney beans
- 3 lb. tomatoes; peeled and chopped.
- 1 tbsp. extra-virgin olive oil
- 1 celery stalk; chopped
- 2 carrots; chopped
- 1 onion; chopped
- 1 tsp. Italian seasoning
- 2 cups baby spinach
- 1 cup corn kernels
- 1 cup asiago cheese, grated

- 2 tbsp. basil; chopped
- 1 zucchini; chopped
- 4 garlic cloves; minced.
- 1 cup uncooked pasta
- Salt and black pepper to the taste

**DIRECTIONS:**
1. Set your instant pot on Sauté mode; add oil and heat it up.
2. Add onion, stir and cook for 5 minutes
3. Add carrots, garlic, celery, corn and zucchini, stir and cook 5 minutes.
4. Add tomatoes, stock, Italian seasoning, pasta, salt and pepper; then stir well. seal the instant pot lid and cook at High for 4 minutes.
5. Release the pressure naturally for 15 minutes, then release remaining pressure by turning the valve to 'Venting', carefully open the lid; add beans, basil and spinach
6. Add more salt and pepper if needed, divide into bowls, add cheese on top and serve

**NUTRITION:** Calories: 156 Fat: 5 g Protein:1 g

## 79. **Sweet Potato and Turkey Soup**

Preparation Time: 10-20 minutes
Cooking Time: 35 minutes
Servings: 4

**INGREDIENTS:**
- 1 lb. Italian turkey sausage; chopped
- 1 yellow onion; chopped.
- 5 cups turkey stock
- 2 garlic cloves; minced.
- 1 tsp. red pepper flakes
- 1 tsp. basil; dried
- 1 tsp. oregano; dried
- 2 celery stalks; chopped
- 1 tsp. thyme; dried
- 5 oz. spinach; chopped.
- 2 bay leaves
- 2 carrots; chopped
- 1 big sweet potato, cubed
- Salt and black pepper to the taste

**DIRECTIONS:**
1. Set your instant pot on Sauté mode; add sausage, brown it and transfer to a plate
2. Add onion, celery and carrots, stir and cook for 2 minutes
3. Add potato, stir and cook 2 minutes
4. Add stock, garlic, red pepper, salt, pepper, basil, oregano, thyme, spinach and bay leaves,
5. Stir, seal the instant pot lid and cook at High for 4 minutes.
6. Release the pressure naturally for 15 minutes, then release remaining pressure by turning the valve to 'Venting', carefully open the lid; discard bay leaves, divide soup into bowls and serve.

**NUTRITION:** Calories: 240 Fat: 4 g Protein: 8 g

## 80. Endive Soup

Preparation Time: 10-20 minutes
Cooking Time: 45 minutes
Servings: 4

**INGREDIENTS:**

- 6 cups veggie stock
- 1 tbsp. canola oil
- 2 tsp. sesame oil
- 1 tbsp. ginger, grated
- 1 tsp. chili sauce
- 1/2 cup uncooked rice
- 2 scallions; chopped.
- 1 ½ tbsp. soy sauce
- 3 endives, trimmed and roughly chopped
- 3 garlic cloves chopped
- Salt and white pepper to the taste

**DIRECTIONS:**

1. Set your instant pot on Sauté mode; add canola and sesame oil and heat it up
2. Add scallions and garlic, stir and cook for 4 minutes.
3. Add chili sauce and ginger, stir and cook for 1 minute
4. Add stock and soy sauce, stir and cook for 2 minutes.
5. Add rice; then stir well. seal the instant pot lid and cook at High for 15 minutes
6. Release the pressure naturally for 15 minutes, then release remaining pressure by turning the valve to 'Venting', carefully open the lid; add salt, pepper and endives; then stir well. seal the instant pot lid and cook at High for 5 minutes.
7. Release the pressure again, carefully open the lid; stir soup, divide into bowls and serve

**NUTRITION:** Calories: 175 Fat: 5 g Protein: 8 g

## Snacks

### 81. Buns With Carrots And Nuts
Preparation time: 5 minutes.
Cooking time: 20 minutes.
Servings: 4
**INGREDIENTS:**
- ½ cup whole-grain flower
- ¼ cup of sugar
- ½ tsp baking soda
- ¼ tsp cinnamon
- ⅛ tsp nutmeg
- ½ cup grated carrots
- 2 tbsp chopped walnuts
- 2 tbsp grated coconut
- 2 tbsp golden raisins
- 1 egg
- 1 tbsp milk
- ½ tsp vanilla essence
- ¼ cup applesauce

**DIRECTIONS:**
1. Preheat the fryer to a temperature of 350°F. Grease the bottom of 4 muffin molds or glass cups for custard, or magazine with muffin papers. Combine flour, sugar, baking soda, cinnamon, and nutmeg in a medium bowl. Add carrots, nuts, coconut, and raisins to the flour mixture.
2. Beat together the egg, milk, and vanilla in a small bowl. Add the applesauce. Put the flour mixture and stir until well incorporated.
3. Fill the prepared molds or cups with an equal amount of dough (⅓ cup) and then put them inside the basket. Cook for 15 minutes, then let them cool in the molds for 5 minutes before removing.

**NUTRITION:** Calories: 195 Fat: 11.04g Carbohydrates: 24.25g Protein: 2.22g

### 82. Eggplant Milanese
Preparation time: 5 minutes.
Cooking time: 40 minutes.
Servings: 2
**INGREDIENTS:**
- 1 medium eggplant
- 1 tbsp of vinegar
- 2 lightly beaten whole eggs
- 1 cup of tea flour
- 1 ½ cup breadcrumbs

**DIRECTIONS:**
1. Wash the eggplants and cut into slices of 1 cm maximum thickness, place the slices in a bowl with water and vinegar and let them soak for at least 15 minutes.
2. Preheat the air fryer. Set the time of 5 minutes and the temperature to 200 degrees.
3. Remove water from eggplant slices and place on a roasting pan, sprinkle salt to taste. Pass each slice through the flour, then through the beaten egg and finally in breadcrumbs and squeezing the fingers and hands, so they remain very compact.

4. Place the eggplant slices in the basket of the air fryer and set the timer for 18 minutes and press the power button. Open the time in half to see if the weather needs an adjustment because the eggplants should be crispy on the outside and soft on the inside.

**NUTRITION:** Calories: 103 Fat: 5.61g Carbohydrates: 11.61g Protein: 2.4g

## 83. **Chicken Sandwich**

Preparation time: 5 minutes.
Cooking time: 15 minutes.
Servings: 2
**INGREDIENTS:**

- 2 cloves garlic
- Fresh parsley leaves
- 500g chopped breast
- 1 tsp Salt
- Pepper
- 1 egg L
- 50g milk
- 50g Cheese spread
- 14-16 slices sliced bread
- 7-8 slices semi-cured cheese

**DIRECTIONS:**

1. Chop the garlic and parsley.
2. Add the breast in pieces, salt, and pepper
3. Add the rest of the ingredients and spread slices!
4. Spread the paste on all the slices, cover half with a slice of cheese, and cover with another slice, cut into triangles and there are two options, pass them by egg and breadcrumbs
5. Preheat the 2200C air fryer, about 8 or 10 minutes, until the bread becomes colored.

**NUTRITION:** Calories: 215 Fat: 29.4g Carbohydrates: 38.7g Protein: 24.1g Assume: 0g

## 84. **Potato Balls Stuffed with Ham and Cheese**

Preparation time: 5 minutes.
Cooking time: 25 minutes.
Servings: 4
**INGREDIENTS:**

- 4 potatoes
- 100g cooked ham
- 100g of grated or grated cheese
- Salt
- Ground pepper
- Flour
- Oil

**DIRECTIONS:**

1. Peel the potatoes and cut into quarters.
2. Put in a pot with water and bring to the fire, let cook until tender.
3. Drain and squeeze with a fork until the potatoes are made dough and season.
4. Add the ham and cheese.
5. Let's link everything.
6. Make balls and pass through the flour.
7. Spray with oil and go to the basket of the air fryer.

8. Select 20 minutes, 2000C for each batch of balls you put. Do not pile up because they would break down. From time to time remove from the basket so that they are made on all sides, you have to shake the basket so that the balls roll a little and serve.

**NUTRITION:** Calories: 224 Fat: 14g Carbohydrates: 19g Protein: 4g Sugar: 1g

## 85. Spring Rolls

Preparation time: 5 minutes.
Cooking time: 30 minutes.
Servings: 6
**INGREDIENTS:**

- 8 sheets of Philo pasta
- 2 onions
- 2 carrots
- 1 piece of Chinese cabbage
- 75g of bean sprouts
- Salt
- Ground pepper
- Extra virgin olive oil
- 1 dash of soy sauce

**DIRECTIONS:**

1. Grate the carrots, cabbage, and onions.
2. Put in the Wok some extra virgin olive oil.
3. When it's hot, add the vegetables,
4. Season and sauté without losing the crunchy touch.
5. Incorporate the bean sprouts and the soy sauce.
6. Sauté and let temper so that the Philo pasta does not get very wet.
7. Extend the sheets, distribute the filling between the layers and roll up, in the form of a roll, that is, the filling in the center of the sheet. Give the first fold from the bottom up, then the sides mount them on top of each other, and now you end up spinning up its width.
8. Place in the basket of the air fryer, 2 in 2.
9. Paint with oil.
10. Select 20 minutes, 1800C.
11. Make all the rolls.
12. When you have them all done, place all in the basket of the air fryer, one over the other carefully. Select 5 minutes, 1800C, and give a heat stroke so that all are served hot.

**NUTRITION:** Calories: 105 Fat: 10g Carbohydrates: 3g Protein: 5g Sugar: 0g

## 86. Mini Burgers

Preparation time: 5 minutes.
Cooking time: 25 minutes.
Servings: 4
**INGREDIENTS:**

- 500g Minced pork
- Salt
- Ground pepper
- Garlic Powder
- Fresh parsley
- Spices
- 1 egg

- 1 tbsp grated bread
- Mini Bread for Burgers

**DIRECTIONS:**

1. Dress the meat of the hamburgers.
2. Add some salt to the ground beef, some ground pepper, garlic powder, a tablespoon of chopped fresh parsley, a teaspoon of spices.
3. Now, throw an egg and one or two teaspoons of breadcrumbs, so that the meat becomes more consistent. Stir all ingredients well until everything is integrated
4. Then, cover it with transparent and let it rest in the refrigerator for at least half an hour or more. It will be easier after handling the meat and giving it the shape of a hamburger.
5. Once the time has elapsed, take out the meat. Take it out of the paper that surrounds the container and begins to mold and make the mini burger.
6. To prepare them in the fryer:
7. First, heat the fryer. So, adjust the thermostat to 2000C and the timer for about 5 minutes. When it is hot, the pilot or the green light will go out.
8. When half the time has passed, turn around so that they are done well by both parties.

**NUTRITION:** Calories: 219 Fat: 17g Carbohydrates: 0g Sugar: 0g Protein: 18g

## 87. Sausages And Chorizos

Preparation time: 10 minutes.
Cooking time: 20 minutes.
Servings: 2-4

**INGREDIENTS:**

- 300g of sausage or frozen sausages
- One tablespoon olive oil

**DIRECTIONS:**

1. Remove sausages directly from the freezer and place them in the fryer basket.
2. To defrost sausages and remove some of their fat, you must boil them for 5 to 10 minutes, and then prick food to remove all the remaining fat.
3. Then separate the sausages and chorizos on a tray or bowl.
4. Add a tablespoon of your favorite oil (preferably olive oil) in the bowl and mix the sausage well with the oil.
5. Then place the sausages and chorizos in the fryer basket.
6. Program your fryer at a temperature of 190°C and the timer in about 10 minutes.
7. Then turn the sausage as well as chorizos and perform the same process with the fryer.
8. And finally, after 10 minutes, serve and enjoy them.

**NUTRITION:** Calories: 356 Fat: 29.30g Carbohydrates: 1.90g Protein: 21.18g

## 88. Sausage Puff Pastry

Preparation time: 5 minutes.
Cooking time: 20 minutes.
Servings: 1-4

**INGREDIENTS:**

- Amount needed of puff pastry
- Amount needed of sausages

**DIRECTIONS:**

1. Cut the puff pastry into thin slices about 5 cm wide.
2. Divide the sausages into two pieces.
3. Preheat the air fryer a few minutes at 1800C.
4. Meanwhile, roll each piece of sausage with a strip of puff pastry and paint on top with beaten egg.

5. Place in the basket of the air fryer.
6. Set the timer 10 minutes at 1800C temperature.
7. Take as an appetizer at any time of the year. Kids love it.

**NUTRITION:** Calories: 135 Fat: 11g Carbohydrates: 5g Protein: 4g

## 89. Flank Steak with Balsamic Mustard

Preparation time: 10 minutes.
Cooking time: 2h 15 minutes.
Servings: 3

**INGREDIENTS:**

- 60 ml of olive oil
- 60 ml balsamic vinegar
- 36g Dijon mustard
- 16 oz flank steak
- Salt and pepper to taste
- 4 basil leaves, sliced

**DIRECTIONS:**

1. Mix olive oil, balsamic vinegar, and mustard. Mix them to create a marinade.
2. Put the steak directly in the marinade. Cover with plastic wrap and marinate in the fridge for 2 hours or at night.
3. Remove from the refrigerator and let it reach room temperature.
4. Preheat the air fryer by pressing Start/Pause.
5. Place the fillet in the preheated air fryer, select Fillet, and press Start/Pause.
6. Cut the steak at an angle through the muscle. Season with salt and pepper and decorate with the basil to serve.

**NUTRITION:** Calories: 275 Fat: 6.1g Carbohydrates: 18.8g Protein: 29.5g

## 90. Pine Skewers Aceto Reduction

Preparation time: 5 minutes.
Cooking time: 15 minutes.
Servings: 2

**INGREDIENTS:**

- 1 small can of pineapple in its juice
- Necessary quantity Peeled prawns
- Skewers Sticks
- For the sauce:
- 150 ml of Balsamic Aceto
- 120g of sugar

**DIRECTIONS:**

1. Open a small can of pineapple in its juice and drain well.
2. Cut the pineapple slices into four parts and set aside.
3. Peel the prawns and take out the tail.
4. Preheat the air fryer at 1800C temperature for a few minutes and put the skewers in the basket. Program the timer about 10 minutes at 18000C.
5. To prepare the balsamic Aceto sauce: place the Aceto and sugar in a small pot. Reduce over low heat until it thickens but without letting caramel.
6. Let stand until it cools.

**NUTRITION:** Calories: 226g Fat: 2g Carbohydrates: 36g Proteins: 16g

# Desserts

## 91. Fried Cream

Preparation Time: 10-20 minutes
Cooking Time: 15-30 minutes
Servings: 8
**INGREDIENTS:**
**For the cream:**

- 500 ml of whole milk
- 3 egg yolks
- 150 g of sugar
- 50 g flour
- 1 envelope Vanilla Sugar
- Ingredients for the pie:
- 2 eggs
- Unlimited Breadcrumbs
- 1 tsp oil

**DIRECTIONS:**

1. First prepare the custard; once cooked, pour the cream into a dish previously covered with a transparent film and level well. Let cool at room temperature for about 2 hours.
2. Grease the basket and distribute it all over.
3. When the cream is cold, place it on a cutting board and cut it into dice; Pass each piece of cream first in the breadcrumbs, covering the 4 sides well in the beaten egg and then in the pie.
4. Place each part inside the basket. Set the temperature to 1500C.
5. Cook for 10 to 12 minutes, turning the pieces after 6 to 8 minutes.
6. The doses of this cream are enough to make 2 or even 3 kitchens in a row.

**NUTRITION:** Calories: 355 Fat: 18.37g Carbohydrates: 44.94g Sugars: 30.36g Protein: 4.81g

## 92. Italian cake

Preparation Time: 10-20 minutes
Cooking Time: 30-45 minutes
Servings: 8
**INGREDIENTS:**

- 250g of potato starch
- 150g of flour 00 (flour 55)
- 250g of sugar
- 6 eggs
- 50 g butter
- 1 sachet of yeast
- Powdered sugar

**DIRECTIONS:**

1. Melt the butter in a small saucepan and let it cool.
2. Beat the eggs with the fine sugar until you get a light and frothy mixture. Add the flour, starch, sifted yeast, melted butter and mix until a homogeneous mixture is obtained.
3. Butter and flour the basket and pour the preparation into it.
4. Set the temperature to 1800C and cook the cake for 35 min.
5. Remove the cake from the bowl, let it cool and sprinkle with icing sugar.

**NUTRITION:** Calories: 440 Carbohydrates: 40g Fat: 30g Sugars: 28g Protein: 4g

## 93. Apple Rotation

Preparation Time: 10 – 20 minutes
Cooking Time: 15 – 30 minutes
Servings: 6
**INGREDIENTS:**

- 1 roll of rectangular puff pastry
- 220g of apples
- 50g of sugar
- 100g raisins
- 50g pine nuts
- To taste breadcrumbs
- Cinnamon powder to taste

**DIRECTIONS:**

1. Put the raisins in warm water for at least 30 min. Meanwhile, peel the apples, remove the kernel, and cut them into thin slices. Pour the apples into a large bowl and add the dried raisins.
2. Add the cinnamon, sugar, and pine nuts, gently mix the ingredients and let stand.
3. Meanwhile, spread the puff pastry on a work surface with parchment paper. Sprinkle with the breadcrumbs, leaving a 2-3 cm border around. Place the mixture in the center of the dough and close the coating along.
4. Be careful not to tear the dough, close the sides tightly so that the contents do not come out during cooking.
5. Place the liner on the air fryer and Cook over low temperature for about 25 min. When finished cooking, sprinkle the strudel with icing sugar and serve warm sliced.

**NUTRITION:** Calories: 411 Fat: 19.38g Carbohydrates: 57.5g Sugars: 50g Protein: 3.72g

## 94. Stuffed brioche crown

Preparation Time: more than 30 minutes
Cooking Time: 30 – 45 minutes
Servings: 8
**INGREDIENTS:**

- 250g Manitoba flour
- 250g flour 00
- 200 ml of warm milk
- 100 ml of warm water
- 50 ml of olive oil
- 25g baker's yeast
- 1 tbsp sugar
- 1 tsp fine salt
- 250g cooked ham
- 8 slices of emmental cheese
- Poppy seeds
- 1 tbsp of water
- 1 tsp olive oil

**DIRECTIONS:**

1. Prepare the brioche crown and let it grow in a lightly floured and closed container with food wrap for about an hour.

2. Once the survey is finished, spread the dough with a rolling pin, forming a narrow rectangle. First place the ham and then the cheese, leaving about 2 cm of free edge around.

3. Roll everything up to get a cylinder. Cut approximately 2 cm slices and place them in the basket covered with baking paper by placing them side by side to form a crown.

4. Let the preparation rise for another hour before cooking. In the end, brush with a mixture of warm water and oil over the entire surface of the crown and sprinkle with poppy seeds.

5. Preheat the air fryer at 1800C for 5 minutes. Cook for 40 minutes.

**NUTRITION:** Calories: 516 Fat: 32g Carbohydrates: 39g Sugars: 7g Protein: 17g

## 95. Nut cake

Preparation Time: 10-20 minutes
Cooking Time: 30-45 minutes
Servings: 10

**INGREDIENTS:**

- 250 g of walnuts
- 150g Maïzena
- 4 medium eggs
- 200g of butter (room temperature)
- 1 sachet of yeast
- 1 sachet of vanilla sugar
- 200g of sugar

**DIRECTIONS:**

1. Chop the nuts with 50 g of sugar. Using a food processor, beat the butter with the remaining sugar until you get a shiny and foamy mixture.
2. Add the eggs one by one, making sure the mixture is still soft, then add the vanilla.
3. Add the chopped nuts with the sugar and then the cornstarch that will sift with the yeast.
4. Butter and flour the basket, then pour the mixture in the center.
5. Set the air fryer at 1800C.
6. Cook for 45 minutes (turn off the lower heating element 40 minutes later). Let cool before serving.

**NUTRITION:** Calories: 440 Fat: 20.48g Carbohydrate 62.22g Sugars: 49.65g Protein: 3.72g

## 96. Genoise Cake

Preparation Time: 10-20 minutes
Cooking Time: 30-45 minutes
Servings: 10

**INGREDIENTS:**

- 6 eggs
- 190g of sugar
- 150g of flour 00 (flour 55)
- 75g potato starch
- 2g vanilla sugar

**DIRECTIONS:**

1. In a bowl, beat the eggs with the sugar until you get a light and smooth mixture. Add the sifted flour, starch and vanilla sugar and mix with a whisk until a homogeneous mixture is obtained.
2. Butter and flour the basket, then pour the mixture.
3. Set the air fryer to 1800C and simmer for 35 minutes.

**NUTRITION:** Calories: 74 Fat:1.83g Carbohydrate10.91g Sugars: 5.08g Protein: 3.83g

## 97. Frozen Sorrentino gnocchi

Preparation Time: 10-20
Cooking Time: 0 – 15 minutes
Servings: 2
**INGREDIENTS:**

- 550 g Sorrentino gnocchi

**DIRECTIONS:**

1. Pour the gnocchi in the basket and cook for 13 minutes at 1500C mixing once halfway through cooking.

**NUTRITION:** Calories: 170 Carbohydrates: 30g Fat: 2g Sugars: 11g Protein: 6g

## 98. Khachapuri (Georgian bread)

Preparation Time: more than 30 minutes
Cooking Time: 15 – 30 minutes
Servings: 4
**INGREDIENTS:**

- 500g of flour
- 450g whole yogurt
- ½ tsp baking soda
- ½ tsp salt
- 150 g ricotta
- 100g provokes smoked
- 150g Greek feta cheese
- 4 tbsp fine parsley

**DIRECTIONS:**

1. Prepare the khachapuri dough by mixing all the ingredients until a smooth and homogeneous mixture is obtained. Divide the dough into 8 equal parts.
2. Form 8 balls cover them with a clean cloth. Let them rest in a warm place and away from drafts. After about 1 hour of lifting, start spreading the dough.
3. Meanwhile, prepare the filling by grating provokes smoked and the feta cheese and then mix with the ricotta and parsley.
4. Spread the 8 balls by hand in circles of 10 to 15 cm, fill 4 circles with the previously prepared filling and close with the other 4. Now roll the 4 khachapuri with a roller until you get a diameter of the size of the basket.
5. Grease the bottom of the basket and place 1 khachapuri. Also grease the surface and prick with a fork.
6. Set the air fryer to 1800C and cook each khachapuri for 15 minutes.

**NUTRITION:** Calories: 556 Fat: 33g Carbohydrates: 37g Sugars: 3.6g Protein: 28g

## 99. Marble cake

Preparation Time: 10-20 minutes
Cooking Time: 45-60 minutes
Servings: 10
**INGREDIENTS:**

- 190g Butter
- 1g bag of vanilla sugar
- 12g baking powder
- 375g Flour
- 22g cocoa powder

- 4g medium eggs
- 225g of sugar
- 165 ml of milk
- Salt (a pinch)

**DIRECTIONS:**

1. Put the previously softened butter into small pieces in a bowl with the sugar, mount the ingredients until a white and foamy cream forms.
2. Add the eggs at room temperature, one by one, the salt and beat about 5 minutes until you get a mixture without lumps. Add the flour (except 30 g that will keep aside), the yeast and vanilla sugar sifted alternately with the milk.
3. Mix the ingredients well, then divide them evenly and add the remaining flour in a bowl and the sifted cocoa in another.
4. Butter and flour the basket and first place the transparent mixture divided into three separate parts. Do the same with the dark mixture by filling the remaining gaps between the light mixture.
5. To get the veined effect, rotate a fork from top to bottom through the two colors of the mixture.
6. Set the air fryer to 1800C and cook for 40 minutes and then turn off the lower resistance.
7. Cook for another 10 min. Control the baking of the cake with the tip of a knife.

**NUTRITION:** Calories: 195 Fat: 7.6g Carbohydrates: 28g Sugars: 14g Protein: 3.5g

## 100.  **Apple, cream, and hazelnut crumble**

Preparation Time: 10-20 minutes
Cooking Time: 15-30 minutes
Servings: 6

**INGREDIENTS:**

- 4 golden apples
- 100 ml of water
- 50g cane sugar
- 50g of sugar
- ½ tbsp cinnamon
- 200 ml of fresh cream
- Chopped hazelnuts to taste

**DIRECTIONS:**

1. In a bowl, combine the peeled apples, cut into small cubes, cane sugar, sugar, and cinnamon.
2. Pour the apples inside the basket, add the water. Set the air fryer to 1800C and simmer for 15 minutes depending on the type of apple used and the size of the pieces.
3. At the end, divide the apples in the serving glasses, cover with previously whipped cream and sprinkle with chopped hazelnuts.

**NUTRITION:** Calories: 828.8 Fat: 44.8 g Carbohydrate 120.6 g Sugars:54.2 g Protein:4.4 g

# Conclusion

This Omni Air fryer Cookbook contains easy, delicious and healthy recipes that can be prepared within few minutes. It is highly recommended for people with busy schedules and also for those on Weight Watchers Program.

Even if you have never tried the Air Fryer before, I can promise you one thing, after the 30 days, you will be kicking yourself for having not discovered this sooner.

I hope it was able to inspire you to clean up your kitchen from all the useless appliances that clutter your countertop and start putting the Air Fryer to good use. I also hope that your air fryer is giving you lots of joy, time and most importantly, tasty dishes. Please feel free to adjust and alter these recipes, or simply use them as a springboard of inspiration for your own creations!

The Air Fryer is definitely a change in lifestyle that will make things much easier for you and your family. You'll discover increased energy, decreased hunger, a boosted metabolism and of course a LOT more free time! Now you know that Air fryer ovens are no less than a kitchen miracle, which have significantly brought ease and convenience with their user-friendly control systems, time and energy-efficient heating mechanism, and multiplicity of the cooking options. In this cookbook, the author has managed to share as many as different recipes, to provide an extensive guideline to all the frequent oven users. With its latest technology, you can bake, air fry, broil, dehydrate, toast, and roast all sorts of the meal, whether it is your morning breakfast or range of seafood, poultry, pork, beef, lamb, and vegetables. Give it a full read and find out tons of new ways to add more colors and flavors to your dinner table using the latest Omni Air fryer ovens.

Putting together interesting and unexpected ingredients is so much fun and can be really rewarding, so get creative in your kitchen.

Always remember to clean your air fryer and accessories according to the instructions and safety precautions after each cooking adventure.

Like every appliance, maintenance is needed to get what you would like in the device. Any tool employed for preparing food must be stored spotlessly clean. Don't let dirt develop and clean the environment fryer frequently so you get great results any time you make use of the air fryer. You have to make certain you retain it keep clean and maintain it for results efficiently along with a taken care of appliance always lasts longer. We provide you with some cleanings tips, however it is not difficult. The outdoors and inside parts could be cleaned fairly easily and ought to be done frequently. Within the situation from the heating coil, get it done a couple of occasions annually only.

Why use an air fryer?

First and foremost, the air fryer became popular for its numerous health benefits. The convenience and ease of use area close second and this combination make it an easy choice for those who want a healthy, delicious meal in a fraction of the time. For those who doubt the air fryer capabilities and prefer conventional cooking methods, perhaps the following points will be enough to convince them to make the switch to efficient cooking

A massive reduction in oil – no more than a tsp or two of foil is needed to cook food in an air fryer and yet it still achieves the same texture. A far cry from the many cups of oil that you would have to use to cook food in a deep fryer. The result is food that is not soaked in unhealthy fat that will clog the arteries

Easy press-and-go operation – No longer do you need to watch over your frying pan on your stove while frying your food. This also means no splattering of oil and accidental burns. All of the magic happens in the cooking chamber, just set your cooking preferences, push the right button, and let the air fryer do all of the work.

Bursting with flavor – the flavor of the food truly comes out in an air fryer. Despite the small amount of oil used in "frying" the food, the "fried" taste and texture is achieved

Cleaning made Easy – With food baskets that are dishwasher safe, it's as simple as removing it and putting it in. The cooking chamber can easily be cleaned with a cloth and a mild dishwashing soap

Safe – Its components are food safe and the cooking process itself helps you avoid kitchen accidents that can result in oil burns. The body of the air fryer hardly gets hot even if the temperature inside is at its highest.

Using your standard kitchen gloves will give you more than enough protection when handling this kitchen appliance

Versatile unmatched – this modern appliance is more than just a fryer. You can bake, grill, and broil in it too. More of a highly versatile, mini convection oven rather than a fryer

Rapid cooking times – The high temperatures that are circulated in the cooking chamber cut common cooking times in half. This is because the heat is maintained throughout the time being cooked meaning you do not have to worry about the loss of heat slowing down your cooking

These benefits make air fryers the obvious choice when it comes to healthy cooking No compromise on flavor or convenience!

With those many recipes and a comprehensive guideline about the instant pot air fryer crisp, now you know how to put to its best use and enjoy a range of flavorsome crispy meals in no time. This ten in one multipurpose kitchen miracle has brought much-wanted peace and comfort to the lives of the homemakers who can now cook a healthy and delicious meal for their family, in no time. The different segment of this book provides a step by step method to cook a variety of meals ranging from breakfast, poultry, meat, vegetarian, snacks and much more. Get this latest hit of the instant pot series and bring convenience to your kitchen floor now. If you had an air fryer and didn't know what to cook in it, now you do – with all the recipes to for your breakfast, lunch, dinner, and desserts.

What are you still waiting for? Start cooking in your air fryer and enjoy all the foods you thought were not healthy!

Made in the USA
Middletown, DE
12 August 2020